# FOOLPROOF COOKING

# FOOLPROOF COOKING

# MARY BERRY

BBC
BOOKS

1 3 5 7 9 10 8 6 4 2

BBC Books, an imprint of Ebury Publishing
20 Vauxhall Bridge Road,
London SW1V 2SA

BBC Books is part of the Penguin Random House group of companies whose addresses can be found
at global.penguinrandomhouse.com

Copyright © Mary Berry 2016

Photography by Georgia Glynn Smith

This book is published to accompany the television series entitled *Mary Berry's Foolproof Cooking* first
broadcast on BBC Two in 2016. *Mary Berry's Foolproof Cooking* is a Shine TV production.

BBC Commissioning Executive: Tom Edwards
Series Director: David Ambler
Series Producer: Emma Boswell
Executive Producer: Karen Ross
Production Manager: Jane Pelling
Production Co-ordinator: Annie Boutle

First published by BBC Books in 2016

www.eburypublishing.co.uk

A CIP catalogue record for this book is available from the British Library

ISBN 9781785940514

Editorial Director: Lizzy Gray
Project Editor: Kate Fox
Copyeditor: Kate Parker
Food Stylists: Lisa Harrison, Isla Murray
Prop Stylist: Liz Belton
Design: Lucy Stephens
Testing: Lucy Jessop, Emma Franklin, Jan Fullwood, Anne Harnan, Jenna Leiter, Hannah Yeadon
Production: Helen Everson

Colour origination by Altaimage, London
Printed and b                              ardino Druck, Wemding, Germany

Penguin Random House i               sustainable future for our business, our readers and our planet.
This bo     k is made from Forest Stewardship Council® certified paper.

# INTRODUCTION

Cooking for friends and family, whether it's for a speedy supper or a celebratory lunch, should be enjoyable, fun and rewarding. The recipes in this book are just that. They are designed to be foolproof – dishes you can depend on completely, with no worry or panic, making cooking so much more relaxing and pleasurable. All have been tried and tested to work seamlessly, and I hope they will give you the confidence you need to enjoy cooking every day of the week.

Nowadays, we all lead such busy lives that we need to find ways to save time and plan ahead. For this new collection I've made sure that lists of ingredients are kept to a minimum, using store-cupboard staples wherever possible. Turn to page 302 for my suggestions on how to stock your store cupboard and fridge with some useful basics so that you always have something to hand. Used cleverly, the freezer can also help transform the way you cook, allowing you to prepare dishes ahead for special occasions or store leftover suppers for when time is short – see page 304 for my foolproof guide on how to make the most of it.

Preparation is fundamental to becoming a confident cook, whether planning meals for the week ahead or devising a menu for a special celebration. Cooking for the family day to day can actually be more demanding, in my view, partly due to lack of time during the week, but also because of the need to make meals that are healthy and well balanced while keeping an eye on the budget. My handy guide to family cooking (see page 308) offers lots of advice on getting organised to do the best you can midweek. And cooking from scratch doesn't have to be time-consuming; many quick and simple dishes can be knocked up in minutes – like my Express Bacon and Pesto Pasta (page 154), or Beef Stir-fry with Ribbon Vegetables on page 132.

Entertaining friends and family, no matter how small your gathering, can be stressful, but I've always stood by my 'prepare ahead as much as you can' mantra, and it has never failed me. All of the recipes in this collection give guidance on preparing ahead and freezing, where relevant, to make them as practical and helpful as possible. And before you start have a look through my foolproof tips for entertaining on page 310.

Many of the dishes in this new collection are perfect for entertaining, in fact, straightforward to make but guaranteed to go down well. For a super-quick starter, try my Tomato and Basil Salad with Whipped Goat's Cheese and Parma Ham on page 15 – it's so simple to prepare but is a stunning combination. The Butterflied Leg of Lamb with Preserved Lemons on page 151 makes for an impressive main course and takes very little time to prepare – it's marinated ahead to create a wonderful depth of flavour, and can be roasted or barbecued in less than 40 minutes.

If you're craving a hearty Sunday lunch, try the succulent herby roast chicken on page 103 or the Roast Rack of Pork with Sage and Lemon Rub and foolproof crackling on page 122. There are times, of course, when all you want is a hassle-free, all-in-one dish that allows you to put your feet up while the slow cooking does all the hard work for you. You simply can't go wrong with my version of coq au vin on page 100, or, for a true British classic, try my Boiled Beef and Carrots and Mustard Parsley Sauce on page 126 – a real favourite of mine that my mother passed on to me.

While I love meat, and regard it as an important part of a balanced diet, fish makes a lovely, lighter alternative to meat. Salmon is such a straightforward fish to cook – try my Spiced, Blackened Salmon on page 62. The Whole Sea Bass with Lime and Dill Butter on page 65 makes a wonderful combination and shows how a simple herb or spiced butter can instantly add an extra dimension to a dish.

I've particularly enjoyed creating recipes for the Salads and Vegetables chapter of this new collection. I find global cuisine so inspirational, especially when it comes to meat-free cooking: my Oriental Vegetable and Noodle Salad with Ginger on page 176 is packed with flavour and so versatile – you could add cooked fish or meat, if you preferred, or simply serve it on its own as a light lunch or supper. For more meat-free options, why not try my Creamy Roasted Pepper Pasta with Feta and Olives (page 166) or the Middle Eastern Aubergine and Chickpea Salad on page 181 with its touch of spice and beautifully contrasting textures.

No cookbook of mine would be complete without at least a couple of chapters on sweet things. I can always find an excuse to make a pudding! For me an indulgent pud rounds off a meal perfectly, whether it's a childhood favourite or a British winter classic to end a lazy Sunday lunch – like my Brioche Bread and Butter Pudding (page 240) – or, a lighter, more elegant dessert to provide a stunning finish to a dinner party, for which the Mango, Lemon and Lime Mousse on page 215 would be ideal. Whichever direction your sweet tooth takes you, making a pudding is always so rewarding and the results are well worth the effort. If you're entertaining for large numbers or making multiple courses for a dinner party, it's always wise to opt for a chilled or frozen dessert that can be prepared at least a day in advance, like my decadent Passion Fruit Pots on page 212 – a lovely twist on lemon posset and ever so moreish. There are also a handful of frozen puddings that are excellent to have on standby: Real Honeycomb Ice Cream on page 225 is bound to be popular and my Ginger Semifreddo with Poached Pears (page 233) is a really handy cheat's dessert that's speedy to whip up and easy to serve.

Baking is one of the most rewarding and relaxing forms of cooking, and I never tire of making a sweet treat to share with friends and family for afternoon tea or a birthday celebration. I especially love baking with my grandchildren, and my Chocolate and Cherry Biscuits (page 287) and Two-tone Toffee Chews (page 290) are both excellent recipes to make with children – it's great fun getting them involved. If you're after a show-stopper of a cake for a special occasion, you simply must try my Cardamom Sponge with White Chocolate Icing (page 277) – it has just the right level of spice, which offsets the creamy, velvety icing so well.

I've really enjoyed coming up with the recipes for this cookbook and ensuring that they are all foolproof. To add an extra layer of security, I've also included key tips alongside each recipe to help guide you through any trickier techniques and to guarantee success. I'm so thrilled to be sharing these tried and tested recipes with you, and I hope that you will gain as much satisfaction cooking them for friends and family as I've done creating them.

# SHARING PLATTERS & NIBBLES

# HERB FLATBREAD WITH MOZZARELLA AND ASPARAGUS

**You can cook this dough base in different ways: in a frying pan on the hob, on a griddle or even a barbecue – it is a great outdoor option for children. If cooking on the barbecue, just split the flatbreads open and fill with sweetcorn, chopped ham, tomatoes or cheese with sauce. No need for plates!**

Serves 4

PREPARE AHEAD
The flatbread can be made and cooked up to 8 hours ahead, the toppings added up to 4 hours ahead. The dough can be stored in the fridge overnight – bring to room temperature and knead in the herbs before cooking.

## FOR THE HERB DOUGH

175g (6oz) strong white flour, plus extra for dusting

1 tsp fast-action dried yeast

1 tbsp olive oil, plus extra for oiling and frying

150ml (5fl oz) warm water

1 tbsp chopped flat-leaf parsley

1 tbsp chopped basil

salt and freshly ground black pepper

## FOR THE TOPPING

100g (4oz) fine asparagus tips

1 x 125g mozzarella ball, broken into chunks

100g (4oz) sun-blushed tomatoes, drained (if in oil) and halved if large

½ bunch of basil, roughly chopped

balsamic glaze, to serve

1 You will need a large frying pan, at least 28cm (11in) in diameter, or a griddle.

2 To make the dough, measure the flour into a large bowl with the yeast, oil and ½ teaspoon of salt. Pour in the warm water gradually, adding enough to make a soft dough – you may not need to use all the water. Bring the mixture together using your hands (see tip).

3 Tip on to a floured work surface and knead the dough for about 10 minutes until smooth and shiny. Place in an oiled bowl, cover with cling film and leave to rise in a warm place for 1½ hours or until doubled in size.

4 When risen, tip the dough on to a floured work surface and knead for 5–6 minutes before kneading in the chopped parsley and basil. Roll the dough out to form a 28cm (11in) disc.

5 Heat up the frying pan or griddle until hot. Pour in a little oil, then add the dough and fry over a high heat for 4–5 minutes on each side until lightly browned and cooked through.

6 Meanwhile, for the topping, cook the asparagus in boiling salted water for 3–4 minutes, drain and refresh in cold water (see tip on page 184).

7 Sit the flatbread on a board, scatter with the mozzarella, tomatoes, asparagus and basil, drizzle over some balsamic glaze, season with salt and pepper and serve.

## MARY'S FOOLPROOF TIP

The dough just needs to be mixed together before kneading, so if you are making and kneading the dough in a food mixer with a dough hook, be careful not to overwork it.

# TOMATO AND BASIL SALAD WITH WHIPPED GOAT'S CHEESE AND PARMA HAM

This looks stunning as a shared platter, though you could serve it in individual portions if you prefer. Look for firm ripe tomatoes, using as many different varieties as you can for the best effect.

Serves 6

PREPARE AHEAD
Assemble the salad up to 6 hours ahead and pour over the dressing just before serving.

150g (5oz) soft goat's cheese (such as Chavroux)

100ml (3½fl oz) double cream, lightly whipped

1.5kg (3lb) mixed tomatoes (red, brown, green and yellow – such as beefsteak, oxheart, heritage, plum, vine, bush, cherry, Marmande, Losetto, Tumbling Tom Yellow)

4–6 spring onions, sliced on the diagonal

1 handful of small basil leaves, left whole

6 slices of Parma ham

coarse sea salt and freshly ground black pepper

chunky bread, to serve

FOR THE BASIL DRESSING

1 garlic clove, crushed

6 tbsp olive oil

2 tbsp white wine vinegar

1 tsp sugar

1 bunch of basil, chopped

1 Place the goat's cheese and whipped cream in a bowl, season with salt and pepper and mix together. Spoon into a small serving bowl, sit in the centre of a large platter and garnish with a sprig of basil. If making individual plates, put the goat's cheese and cream on a china spoon or in a tiny bowl for each plate.

2 Cut any green and/or yellow tomatoes into thick slices and arrange around the edge of the platter. Cut the remaining (red and/or brown) tomatoes in half or large chunks, depending on their size. Scatter over the platter around the goat's cheese. Scatter the spring onions and basil leaves over the tomatoes and season with black pepper.

3 To make the dressing, add the ingredients to the small bowl of a food processor and whizz until blended. Arrange the Parma ham in swirled slices around the goat's cheese.

4 Just before serving, sprinkle salt over the tomatoes (see tip), pour over the basil dressing and serve with chunky bread.

## MARY'S FOOLPROOF TIP

Do not add salt to the tomatoes too early or they will release too much liquid and lose their flavour.

# PARTY PLOUGHMAN'S

**Great to serve as a sharing platter at a large party, this is all about choosing the very best ingredients (see tip) and presenting them in an attractive way.**

Serves 6–8

PREPARE AHEAD
Prepare the platter up to 8 hours ahead.

150g (5oz) full-flavoured stuffed green olives

12 sun-blushed tomatoes, drained (if in oil) and halved

2 tbsp good olive oil

1 tbsp balsamic vinegar

2 celery sticks, cut into shorter lengths

150g (5oz) mature Cheddar cheese

150g (5oz) Oxford Blue cheese

a square of quince jelly, or 2 tbsp fruit chutney

6 slices of dry-cured ham

6 slices of spiced sausage (such as salami)

6 ripe fresh figs, cut into quarters

1 or 2 bunches of tomatoes on the vine

1 seeded brown loaf, cut into large wedges

1 Place the olives and sun-blushed tomatoes in separate bowls. Pour the olive oil and balsamic vinegar into another bowl.

2 Place the bowls and the celery on a large platter or wooden board with all the remaining ingredients in batches around them.

## MARY'S FOOLPROOF TIP

You do not have to be ruled by the cheeses suggested here. Choose a couple of cheeses that you enjoy and that have different flavours and textures – perhaps a specialist local soft cheese, and a hard cheese with a more mature flavour.

# CONTINENTAL SHARING PLATTER WITH BAKED CAMEMBERT

**Sharing platters like this are great as a starter for a dinner party or for a large gathering – make a few of them to hand round. It's all about presentation – I like to serve everything on a rectangular wooden board, but you could use one made in a more unusual shape. A slate or a large, flat china plate would work equally well too.**

Serves 6

PREPARE AHEAD
Prepare the platter up to 8 hours ahead. The dip can be made up to 3 days ahead and kept chilled in the fridge.

6 slices of Parma ham

6 slices of salami

6 slices of chorizo

200g (7oz) pitted olives

6 sweet cucumber spears with dill from a jar (see tip), each sliced in half lengthways

1 x 250g Camembert cheese in a wooden box

8 small sprigs of rosemary

10 mini pitta breads

FOR THE RED PEPPER DIP

1 x 230g jar of chargrilled red peppers (see tip), drained

1 bunch of basil

200g (7oz) full-fat cream cheese

200g (7oz) mayonnaise

1 garlic clove, halved

juice of 1 lemon

salt and freshly ground black pepper

1 Preheat the oven to 200°C/180°C fan/Gas 6.

2 First make the red pepper dip. Place all the ingredients in a blender or food processor, season with salt and pepper and whizz until smooth. Spoon into a small serving bowl.

3 Take a serving platter or board and sit the dip at one end. Arrange the meats, swirled together, on the platter, then add a bowl of olives and the cucumber spears.

4 Take the Camembert from its box, remove the paper around it and then place it back in the box, without the lid. Stud the top of the cheese with the sprigs of rosemary, place on a baking tray and bake in the oven for about 10 minutes or until runny and hot.

5 Meanwhile, toast the pitta breads in a griddle pan or under the grill, and arrange on the platter with the hot cheese. Serve and dig in!

## MARY'S FOOLPROOF TIP

This recipe is all about speed and cheating! So there is nothing wrong with buying the red peppers and cucumber ready prepared in jars.

# GIANT CHEESE AND PARMA HAM STRAWS

These are lovely on their own, to serve with drinks or to accompany soup or a salad. Full of flavour, they are also quite substantial – no need for more than one per person. You could use Black Forest or Serrano ham, instead of Parma, if they are more easily available. (Pictured overleaf.)

| Makes 6 large cheese straws | PREPARE AHEAD | FREEZE |
|---|---|---|
| | Can be made up to 2 days ahead and reheated in the oven to serve. | Freezes well for up to a month. |

1 x 375g packet of ready-rolled, all-butter puff pastry

plain flour, for dusting

3 tbsp Dijon mustard

75g (3oz) Gruyère cheese, finely grated

4 wafer-thin slices of Parma ham

1 egg, beaten

1 Roll out the pastry on a lightly floured work surface into a rectangle about 25 x 35cm (10 x 14in) and 3mm (⅛in) thick. Using a pastry brush, spread half the mustard over the pastry and sprinkle with two-thirds of the cheese. Press the cheese into the mustard with your hands.

2 Fold the pastry in half, like a book, so the cheese is in the centre, then roll out again – just enough to press the cheese into the pastry and to create a rectangle large enough to accommodate the slices of Parma ham in a single layer on top.

3 Spread over the remaining mustard and lay the Parma ham in a single layer on the top. Fold the ham-covered pastry in half again and roll out just enough to press everything together (see tip). Brush the top with beaten egg and sprinkle over the remaining cheese.

4 Cut the pastry into six long strips. Twist each strip four times to form a cheese straw, then place on the prepared baking sheet (with space between each of the straws as they will expand during cooking) and brush with more of the beaten egg. Place in the fridge to chill for 20 minutes. While the straws are chilling, preheat the oven to 220°C/200°C fan/Gas 7 and line a baking sheet with baking paper.

5 Bake in the oven for about 20 minutes, then turn the temperature down to 160°C/140°C fan/Gas 3 and bake for a further 10 minutes until golden all over and cooked through. Transfer to a wire rack to cool for a few minutes – these are always best served warm.

## MARY'S FOOLPROOF TIP

It is important to press the cheese and ham into the pastry, otherwise it may fall apart when twisting.

# SAUSAGE AND CARAMELISED ONION MINI PASTIES

**Golden, crisp and very tasty, these are like mini Cornish pasties. The filling is so simple to make too. Delicious served warm or at room temperature, they're not too fragile to pack into a lunchbox for a picnic or a welcome bite to sustain you on a long walk.**

| Makes 8 pasties | PREPARE AHEAD | FREEZE |
|---|---|---|
| | Can be made up to 2 days ahead and reheated in a low oven. | The raw pasties freeze well; defrost completely before baking as in the recipe. |

1 tbsp oil

1 large onion, thinly sliced

1 tsp sugar

2 fat sausages

4 sage leaves, finely chopped

1 x 375g packet of ready-rolled, all-butter puff pastry

plain flour, for dusting

1 egg, beaten

salt and freshly ground black pepper

**1** You will need a 10cm (4in) plain pastry cutter.

**2** Heat the oil in a frying pan over a medium heat and fry the onion for 3 minutes, stirring regularly. Cover with a lid, reduce the heat to low and cook for about 15 minutes until the onion is soft but not browned. Add the sugar and fry for a few more minutes or until the onions are caramelised. Tip into a bowl and set aside to cool.

**3** Cut the skin from the sausages and add the meat to the bowl with the onions, followed by the chopped sage leaves. Season with salt and pepper and stir well.

**4** Re-roll the pastry on a lightly floured surface until large enough to cut out eight discs using the pastry cutter. Brush a little beaten egg around the edges of each disc, put a heaped spoonful of sausage meat into the centre and fold over, sealing the edges of the pasty to give a half-moon shape.

**5** Press around the edges of each pasty using the tines of a lightly floured fork (see tip), brush again with beaten egg and place on the prepared baking sheet. Cover with cling film and chill in the fridge for a minimum of 1 hour. While the pasties are chilling, preheat the oven to 200°C/180°C fan/Gas 6 and line a baking sheet with baking paper.

**6** Bake in the oven for about 20 minutes until crisp and golden; best served warm.

## MARY'S FOOLPROOF TIP

It's important to make sure the edges of the pasties are sealed or the filling will bulge out. Dusting the fork with a little flour before using it to press the edges helps stop it sticking to the pastry.

# SMOKED SALMON, AVOCADO AND CUCUMBER CANAPÉS

**These look so smart and pretty – perfect for handing round at a drinks party. The different textures combine beautifully too.**

Makes 20 canapés

PREPARE AHEAD
Can be assembled up to 4 hours ahead and kept chilled in the fridge.

¼ small cucumber
1 ripe avocado
juice of ½ lemon
1 tsp full-fat
  cream cheese
1 tsp hot
  horseradish sauce
100g (4oz) smoked
  salmon slices
4 small red radishes,
  trimmed and
  thinly sliced
a few pea shoot sprigs
freshly ground
  black pepper

1 You will need 20 canapé or cocktail sticks (see tip).

2 Peel the piece of cucumber and slice in half lengthways. Scoop out the seeds and discard, then cut into 20 half-moon-shaped pieces.

3 Peel the avocado and remove the stone. Cut in half horizontally then cut into 20 even-sized pieces, each roughly the same shape as the cucumber slices, and toss in the lemon juice so they are completely coated (see tip).

4 Mix the cream cheese and horseradish sauce together and season with pepper. Cut the smoked salmon slices into 20 long strips (about five strips per slice) and fold each strip to make a concertina.

5 To assemble, put a slice of cucumber on a chopping board and top with a slice of avocado, a folded strip of smoked salmon, a blob of the horseradish mixture and a slice of radish. Thread a cocktail stick through the middle of the canapé to hold it together. Sprinkle with black pepper and place on a serving platter.

6 Repeat to make 20 canapés. Top each canapé with a pea shoot sprig and scatter some around the platter too, if you like. Serve chilled.

## MARY'S FOOLPROOF TIPS

If you use attractive cocktail sticks, you can re-use them by washing them in a hot wash in the dishwasher.

It's very important to coat the avocado in lemon juice or it will go brown. The avocado should be ripe but still firm.

# WATERMELON, FETA AND MINT STACKS

**These look stunning and are so quick to assemble. Lovely Jo, who does my make-up for TV and shoots, gave me the idea for them. Fastened with unusual canapé or cocktail sticks made from wood, bamboo or coloured plastic, they will look very elegant for a special occasion. (See also tips.)**

Makes 20 canapés

PREPARE AHEAD
Can be assembled up to 6 hours ahead and kept chilled in the fridge.

200g (7oz) watermelon
  flesh, deseeded
200g (7oz) feta cheese
20 small fresh
  mint sprigs
juice of ½ lime,
  to serve

1 You will need 20 canapé or cocktail sticks (see tip on page 25).

2 Slice the melon flesh into 20 x 2cm (¾in) cubes and arrange on a board. Cut the feta into 20 x 2cm (¾in) cubes and place one on top of each melon cube.

3 Add a small sprig of mint to each stack and then insert a cocktail stick through the centre of all three to hold them neatly in place. Just before serving, squeeze over the lime juice.

## MARY'S FOOLPROOF TIPS

This is all about quality ingredients and good presentation. Some feta can be a little slimy, so choose a drier version and pat dry with kitchen paper if needed. Buy fresh watermelon and young, fresh, bright green mint sprigs.

Cut the cubes of watermelon and feta to exactly the same size so the stacks look impressive and not haphazard.

# PRAWN AND AVOCADO LETTUCE CUPS

**A new twist on an old favourite, the prawn cocktail. These are great as a sharing platter or they would work well as a starter, served with lemon wedges and brown bread.**

Makes 12 cups or
serves 4 as a starter

PREPARE AHEAD
The prawn mixture can be made up to 4 hours ahead. Assemble the cups up to
3 hours ahead, then prepare and add the avocado just before serving.

3 tbsp crème fraîche

1 heaped tbsp
   sun-dried tomato paste

2 tsp creamed
   horseradish from a jar

juice of 1 lemon,
   plus lemon wedges
   to serve

350g (12oz) small
   cooked peeled prawns

2 Little Gem lettuces

a little paprika,
   for sprinkling

1 ripe avocado

6 cherry
   tomatoes, halved

salt and freshly ground
   black pepper

1 Mix together the crème fraîche, tomato paste, horseradish and 1 tablespoon of the lemon juice in a bowl. Season with salt and pepper. Pat the prawns dry using kitchen paper, then tip into the bowl and mix together.

2 Cut the stem from each of the lettuces and separate the individual leaves (see tip). Arrange them (curved like cups) on a large platter. Fill each cup evenly with the prawn mixture and sprinkle with a little paprika.

3 Halve the avocado and remove the stone, then peel and thinly slice into 18 pieces. Cut the long slices in half to give 36 pieces. Toss in the remaining lemon juice (see tip on page 25).

4 Arrange three slices of avocado on each lettuce cup and top with half a cherry tomato. Sprinkle with black pepper to serve.

## MARY'S FOOLPROOF TIP

If the lettuce leaves are very large, trim them down before arranging on the serving platter.

# ROASTED AUBERGINE AND GARLIC CHILLI DIP

**This dip goes with anything – breadsticks, cheese straws, pitta bread, crudités of vegetables and even cold meats. It has a fiery kick, so reduce the amount of chilli if you prefer a milder flavour.**

Makes 1 bowl

PREPARE AHEAD
Can be made up to a day ahead (see tip) and kept chilled in the fridge.

1 medium aubergine

2–3 fresh green chillies

2 large garlic cloves (unpeeled)

4 spring onions, chopped

200ml (7fl oz) mayonnaise

juice of ½ lemon

salt and freshly ground black pepper

1½ tbsp snipped chives, to serve

**1** Preheat the oven to 200°C/180°C fan/Gas 6.

**2** Prick the aubergine all over with a fork (this prevents the skin from bursting in the oven). Sit it on a baking tray and roast in the oven for 30 minutes. Scatter in the chillies and whole garlic cloves and return to the oven for 20 minutes. Remove from the oven and set aside to cool.

**3** Once cool enough to handle, halve the aubergine and use a spoon to scoop out the flesh before adding to a food processor. Squeeze the roasted garlic cloves from their skins and add to the processor. Peel the skin and remove some of the seeds from the chillies, then add the flesh to the processor.

**4** Add the chopped spring onions to the food processor with the mayonnaise and lemon juice. Season with salt and pepper and whizz until smooth. Taste for seasoning and to check if the dip is hot enough!

**5** Transfer to a serving bowl, sprinkle with the chives and serve cold.

## MARY'S FOOLPROOF TIP

If you are saving the dip to use later, be aware that the flavours will intensify the longer that it is left. You may want to use a little less chilli and garlic if you are making it a day ahead.

# TOASTED NUTS AND SEEDS
# WITH A HINT OF MAPLE

**Delicious with drinks or to sprinkle over a salad to give a bit of crunch. If you prefer, you can use 250g (9oz) mixed seeds instead of the three separate varieties listed below.**

Makes about 550g
(1¼lb)

PREPARE AHEAD
This mixture can be made up to a week ahead and kept in an airtight container.

50g (2oz)
  sesame seeds

100g (4oz)
  pumpkin seeds

100g (4oz)
  sunflower seeds

100g (4oz)
  cashew pieces

100g (4oz) whole
  blanched almonds

100g (4oz) shelled
  pistachio nuts

1 tbsp olive oil

1 tbsp soy sauce

1 tbsp maple syrup

**1** Preheat the oven to 200°C/180°C fan/Gas 6.

**2** Measure all the ingredients into a bowl and mix together. Tip into a large roasting tin and spread out in a single layer (so they are not on top of each other), then roast in the oven for 10–15 minutes, turning once halfway through cooking, until glazed and golden (see tip).

**3** Allow to cool down fully before transferring to an airtight container.

### MARY'S FOOLPROOF TIP

Keep a close eye on the seeds and nuts as they cook because the maple syrup makes them prone to burning!

# BREADS, SOUPS & STARTERS

# CHEESE AND GARLIC TEAR-AND-SHARE SCONES

These deliciously cheesy scones would be lovely for lunch to accompany soup, and a 'tear-and-share' loaf is perfect for informal eating. Using a scone rather than a yeast dough makes them quicker to make too.

| Serves 10–12 | PREPARE AHEAD | FREEZE |
|---|---|---|
| | Can be made up to a day ahead. | Freeze well cooked. |

450g (1lb)
  self-raising flour, plus
  extra for dusting

2 tsp baking powder

2 tsp mustard powder

1 tsp salt

100g (4oz)
  butter, cubed

50g (2oz) Parmesan
  cheese, finely
  grated, plus extra
  for sprinkling

100g (4oz)
  mature Cheddar
  cheese, grated

1 garlic clove, crushed

6 tbsp finely
  snipped chives

2 eggs

about 150ml
  (5fl oz) milk

1 Preheat the oven to 220°C/200°C fan/Gas 7 and line a baking sheet with baking paper.

2 Measure the flour and baking powder into a large bowl with the mustard, salt and butter. Using your fingertips, rub in the butter until the mixture resembles fine breadcrumbs. Add both cheeses with the garlic and chives.

3 Beat the eggs in a jug, adding enough milk to make up to 300ml (10fl oz) of liquid. Gradually add this to the mixture in the bowl and mix together to make a dough (see tip). Tip on to a lightly floured work surface and knead until smooth, then divide into 22 equal-sized balls.

4 Arrange the balls of dough on the prepared baking sheet to form a round with all the balls just touching. Brush with any leftover liquid in the jug and sprinkle with the extra Parmesan.

5 Bake in the oven for 25 minutes until well risen and golden on top and underneath. Serve warm with butter.

## MARY'S FOOLPROOF TIP

A scone dough should be fairly sticky rather than dry. If it is on the wet side, it gives a better rise and the resulting scones are very moist.

# OLIVE AND HERB SODA BREAD

This is the easiest of loaves to make as the bread is leavened with bicarbonate of soda rather than yeast, so no long proving and rising are needed.

Makes 1 loaf

PREPARE AHEAD
Can be made up to a day ahead.

FREEZE
Freezes well cooked.

500g (1lb 2oz) plain flour, plus extra for dusting

1 tsp bicarbonate of soda

1 tsp salt

1 x 284ml carton of buttermilk

200ml (7fl oz) milk

50g (2oz) sun-dried tomatoes, drained and chopped

75g (3oz) pitted green olives, chopped

3 tbsp snipped chives

1 Preheat the oven 220°C/200°C fan/Gas 7 and line a baking sheet with baking paper.

2 Measure all the dry ingredients into a large bowl and mix well. Gradually add the buttermilk and then the milk (see tip), stirring with a wooden spoon to make a sticky dough. Tip on to a lightly floured work surface and bring together using your hands.

3 Add the tomatoes, olives and chives, folding in until roughly incorporated, then shape the dough into a dome about 20cm (8in) in diameter. (Do not knead the dough but just bring it together – see tip.)

4 Sit the loaf on the prepared baking sheet, divide into quarters (cutting halfway through the dough) and sprinkle with flour.

5 Bake in the oven for 30 minutes or until cooked through, golden brown and sounding hollow when tapped on the base. Leave to cool a little on a wire rack. Best served freshly baked and still warm.

## MARY'S FOOLPROOF TIPS

Add the milks separately – do not mix them together first.

Don't knead the dough too much as this will make it tough; just bring it together and shape, treating it like a scone mixture rather than a bread dough.

# FOOLPROOF BREAD

Making bread, like baking cakes, can be very therapeutic. There is something both satisfying and comforting about the simplicity of the ingredients, the gentle processes involved and the delicious smell of a newly baked loaf – not to mention the wonderful flavour and texture that only freshly made bread can have.

**BREAD WITHOUT YEAST**

Many types of bread are made without yeast. Denser in texture, these don't require kneading or resting/proving (see opposite) and are therefore much less time-consuming to make. If you find kneading a chore, then yeast-free breads like my Olive and Herb Soda Bread on page 37 make a delicious alternative to a standard yeasted loaf.

Yeast-free breads tend to use the same raising agents found in other types of baking, such as baking powder, bicarbonate of soda or self-raising flour. Buttermilk, milk and eggs can be used to enrich the dough and to give a soft texture. As these breads contain no yeast, it's important not to overwork the dough, however – in fact, the less handling the better.

**YEASTED BREAD**

The main ingredients of bread are strong flour, yeast, salt and water. Other ingredients can then be added to vary the basic dough: oil or butter can be included to make the bread richer, or sugar to make it sweeter; some loaves are made with a blend of flours to create different textures; and some include different flavourings, from dried fruit, nuts and seeds to herbs and cheese.

*Flour* Use strong bread flour when making bread. This type of flour has more protein in it, which means more gluten can develop during the process of kneading, making the dough stretchy and able to hold more air.

*Yeast* Yeast is needed to make bread rise. When mixed with the flour and water, the yeast gives off carbon dioxide which causes the dough to rise. If you're a beginner, it's best to go for easy-blend or fast-action dried yeast as it is more straightforward to use than fresh yeast and problems are less likely to arise. Ensure you check the expiry date of your yeast before using it.

*Liquid* Water is most frequently used, though sometimes milk or buttermilk may be substituted. Any liquid should be tepid or cold – not too hot or it will kill the yeast. When made with cold liquid, the dough takes a little longer to rise.

*Salt* This is crucial for flavour. It's best to add the salt and the yeast at opposite sides of the mixing bowl, as salt can be harmful to yeast if it comes into direct contact with it. Don't be tempted to skimp on the quantity given in a recipe. It may seem like a lot, but spread throughout a whole loaf of bread, it amounts to only a small quantity per serving.

The process of making a traditional loaf of bread is relatively simple, but there are a number of stages, so you need to make sure you have set aside enough time to complete each one.

**MIXING AND KNEADING**

DO . . .

*Use your hands to mix* This is the most effective way to mix all the ingredients together thoroughly.

*Be careful when adding liquid* Gauging the quantity of liquid to add is something that improves with experience; you just need to bear in mind that recipes can only be a guide because the absorbency of flour can vary. Aim for a sticky dough; if the dough is dry, the baked loaf will be dry too.

*Check the texture* Again, judging how long to knead the dough is something that comes with practice. As a rule, the dough should become smooth, springy and elastic if you have given it enough time.

*Use a food mixer fitted with a dough hook for kneading* This is just a matter of preference; some people find kneading by hand laborious while others enjoy it.

DON'T . . .

*Get hung up on kneading technique* As long as you are constantly working the dough in some way, you will be activating the gluten.

*Use too much flour when kneading* Use only a very minimal amount of flour to lightly dust your work surface. Adding too much will disrupt the balance of ingredients in the dough and dry out your loaf.

**RESTING, PROVING AND SHAPING**

The first time the dough is left to rise is called the resting phase. Then, the bread is 'knocked back' – knocking the air out of the dough before shaping. After the dough is shaped, it is left to rise once more; this second rising stage is known as proving.

DO . . .

*Have patience* Resting the dough is an important stage in the bread-making process and shouldn't be rushed. Although dough rises more quickly in a warm environment, such as a warm kitchen, it will also rise somewhere cool or even in the fridge; it just takes more time. This can work to your advantage if you want to make the dough a day ahead and leave it to rest overnight in the fridge. It will then be ready to shape, prove and bake in the morning.

*Glaze your loaf* If you want your loaf to have a crisp crust, glaze with a little water; for a shiny finish, brush with a little beaten egg yolk.

DON'T . . .

*Forget to grease the tin* If you are baking your loaf in a tin, make sure you thoroughly grease it with butter so that the loaf doesn't stick.

## DO . . .

***Preheat the oven well in advance*** Always bake bread at a high temperature and preheat the baking tray you are using to bake the bread on so that the loaf bakes evenly.

***Create steam in the oven*** Pop a small dish of water in the base of the oven at the same time as the bread. This creates steam while the bread is baking and will help prevent the crust from forming too quickly.

***Check the bread is fully baked*** Tap the base of the loaf; it should sound hollow rather than dense.

***Remove to a wire rack straight away*** It's best to remove the baked bread from the tin as soon as you can; air needs to circulate around the whole loaf as it cools. If left in the tin to cool, it is likely to go soggy.

***Eat when fresh*** Bread is at its very best when eaten freshly made, although it does keep well for a couple of days if stored in a cool place. It can also be frozen but is best used within 4 months of freezing.

## DON'T . . .

***Underbake your loaf*** It is always better to slightly overbake bread than be left with a raw doughy loaf that is inedible, so if in doubt, leave the bread in the oven for a little longer.

# TEN-MINUTE TOMATO SOUP

**A homemade recipe to rival the nostalgic comfort of classic tinned cream of tomato. With no onions to chop or tomatoes to skin, this soup is quick, easy and delicious. In fact, it is one of my favourite family soups, as I always have the ingredients in the cupboard.**

Serves 6–8

PREPARE AHEAD
Can be made up to 3 days ahead.

FREEZE
Freezes well without the milk and cream. Defrost and reheat until piping hot, then stir in the milk and cream before serving.

6 sun-dried tomatoes in oil

2 garlic cloves, crushed

3 x 400g tins of chopped tomatoes

500ml (18fl oz) chicken or vegetable stock

1 tbsp caster sugar

150ml (5fl oz) full-fat milk

150ml (5fl oz) double cream

3–4 tsp fresh basil pesto (see tip)

salt and freshly ground black pepper

**1** Set a large, deep pan over a medium heat and add 1 tablespoon of oil from the sun-dried tomatoes. Add the garlic and stir-fry for a few seconds.

**2** Tip in the sun-dried and tinned tomatoes, add the stock and sugar (see tip) and bring to the boil, stirring all the while. Season with salt and pepper, then cover with a lid, reduce the heat and simmer for 10 minutes.

**3** Remove from the heat and, using a hand blender, blitz the soup in the pan. Stir in the milk and cream and check the seasoning before heating through on the hob.

**4** Serve hot with ½ teaspoon of basil pesto (see tip) swirled on the top of each bowl of soup.

## MARY'S FOOLPROOF TIPS

The sugar brings out the flavour of the tomatoes and helps balance their acidity – sometimes they can be a little bitter.

The basil pesto adds a lovely flavour, but this soup is still very good without it.

# ROASTED BUTTERNUT SQUASH SOUP

**This is no ordinary butternut squash soup. It has added red pepper and ginger, and needs no cream to improve its velvety texture. Roasting the squash, rather than boiling it in a pan, really brings out the flavour too.**

| Serves 8 | PREPARE AHEAD | FREEZE |
|---|---|---|
| | Can be made up to 3 days ahead. | Freezes well for up to 3 months. |

1.5kg (3lb) peeled and deseeded butternut squash, cut into 3cm (1¼in) cubes (see tip)

1 large onion, roughly chopped

2 medium carrots, peeled and chopped

1 red pepper, deseeded and cut into cubes

4 tbsp olive oil

1 tbsp runny honey

5cm (2in) knob of fresh root ginger, peeled and chopped (see tip on page 187)

1.5 litres (2½ pints) vegetable stock

salt and freshly ground black pepper

**1** You will need a 3.5–4-litre (6–7-pint) deep-sided saucepan. Preheat the oven to 200°C/180°C fan/Gas 6.

**2** Tip the prepared squash into a large, resealable freezer bag with the onion, carrots and red pepper. Sprinkle with half the oil, season with salt and pepper and toss everything together until the vegetables are coated. Tip into a large roasting tin and spread out to form a single layer (use two roasting tins if necessary).

**3** Roast in the oven for 40–45 minutes until tender and tinged brown. Drizzle over the honey 5 minutes before the end of cooking.

**4** Place the large, deep-sided saucepan over a medium heat, add the remaining oil and, when it is hot, add the ginger and fry for a minute. Pour in the stock and bring to the boil, then stir in the roasted vegetables and season with salt and pepper.

**5** Remove from the heat and, using a hand blender, whizz the mixture until smooth. Check the seasoning, adding more salt and pepper if necessary. Return to the heat to warm through and serve hot with crusty bread.

## MARY'S FOOLPROOF TIP

Ready-prepared butternut squash can be bought from supermarkets and makes this soup even quicker to prepare. If you grow your own, use young butternut squash as they are easier to peel.

# CHICKEN NOODLE LAKSA

**Laksa is a popular spicy noodle soup in Peranakan cooking – a combination of Chinese and Malay cuisine found in Malaysia, Singapore and Indonesia. Lucinda, who has been testing recipes with us for 15 years, inspired this wonderfully warming soup. The rice noodles make it even more sustaining.**

Serves 4

PREPARE AHEAD
The chicken mixture can be made up to 8 hours ahead and the noodles soaked just before serving.

2 skinless and boneless chicken breasts, sliced into thin strips

100g (4oz) medium rice noodles

3 tbsp sunflower oil

6 spring onions, finely sliced

2 x 400g tins of coconut milk

2 tsp Thai fish sauce

1 lemon grass stalk, bashed (see tip on page 99)

juice of ½ lime

salt and freshly ground black pepper

coriander leaves, to serve

### FOR THE SPICY PASTE

6 spring onions, roughly sliced

1 fresh red chilli, deseeded and chopped

4cm (1½in) knob of fresh root ginger, peeled and grated

2 garlic cloves, crushed

3 tbsp smooth peanut butter

2 tsp lime juice

1 tbsp light muscovado sugar

**1** First make the spicy paste. Place all the ingredients in the small bowl of a food processor and whizz until finely chopped, or grind with a pestle and mortar.

**2** Spoon 2 tablespoons of the paste into a bowl. Add the chicken strips, season with salt and pepper and toss to coat.

**3** Place the rice noodles in a shallow dish and pour over enough boiling water to cover. Leave for 10–15 minutes or until the noodles have softened. Drain and refresh in cold water, then snip into short lengths and set aside.

**4** Heat a large, deep frying pan or a wok over a high heat. Add 2 tablespoons of the sunflower oil and when it is hot, tip in the spicy chicken strips and quickly fry for about 3 minutes until golden all over and just cooked through. Remove with a slotted spoon and set aside.

**5** Heat the remaining oil in the pan or wok (no need to wash it first), add the sliced spring onions and the remaining spicy paste and fry for a minute. Stir in the coconut milk, fish sauce and lemon grass. Bring to the boil, then reduce the heat and simmer for about 5 minutes.

**6** Add the chicken to the soup and simmer for 3–4 minutes. Divide the noodles between four individual heated bowls (see tip). Remove the lemon grass from the chicken soup and add the lime juice. Ladle the soup over the noodles and sprinkle with coriander leaves to serve.

## MARY'S FOOLPROOF TIP

It is easier to place the noodles in the bowls first and ladle the soup over the top to ensure that everyone has the same amount of soup and noodles.

# CURRIED BEETROOT SOUP

**This is dish is perfect if you grow your own beetroot, as I do. If using raw beetroot, you'll need to boil it until tender first. Ready-cooked beetroot works well otherwise – go for the kind in natural juices rather than vinegar though.**

| Serves 6 | PREPARE AHEAD | FREEZE |
|---|---|---|
| | Can be made up to 2 days ahead and reheated to serve. | Freezes well. |

2 tbsp sunflower oil

1 large onion, chopped

750g (1lb 10oz) cooked beetroot, diced

1 tbsp curry powder

1 x 400g tin of full-fat coconut milk (see tip)

450ml (15fl oz) chicken or vegetable stock

finely grated zest and juice of ½ lime

salt and freshly ground black pepper

TO SERVE

a little pouring double cream

sprigs of coriander

**1** Heat the oil in a deep saucepan, add the onion and fry over a medium-high heat, stirring regularly, for about 5 minutes. Add the beetroot and sprinkle in the curry powder, stirring to coat, and cook for 2 minutes.

**2** Add the coconut milk with the stock, lime zest and juice, and season with salt and pepper. Bring just to the boil, then cover with a lid, reduce the heat and simmer for about 10 minutes or until the beetroot is very tender.

**3** Remove from the heat and, using a hand blender, blitz the soup in the pan until smooth. Return to the hob, bring back to a simmer and check the seasoning. Ladle into warmed soup bowls and serve garnished with a swirl of cream and a sprig of coriander.

## MARY'S FOOLPROOF TIP

Use full-fat coconut milk; the low-fat version is too thin and would give the soup less flavour.

# CRAYFISH MARINIÈRE ON SOURDOUGH

This American recipe was inspired by the crayfish catching I did as part of the TV series that accompanies this book. Crayfish are in abundance in our canals and can be a pest as they breed in huge numbers. You need a licence, which is free, to catch them. If you have not caught your own, you can buy crayfish tails from all good fishmongers or large supermarkets.

Serves 6

2 tbsp olive oil

a knob of butter

1 onion, finely chopped

2 garlic cloves, crushed

200g (7oz) button mushrooms, halved

420g (15oz) shelled crayfish tails

150ml (5fl oz) pouring double cream

25g (1oz) Parmesan cheese, finely grated

juice of ½ small lemon

2 tsp snipped chives

2 tsp chopped dill

salt and freshly ground black pepper

TO SERVE

6 thick slices of sourdough or soda bread (see page 37)

a few salad leaves

6 thin lemon wedges

1 Heat a frying pan until hot, add the oil and butter and, when the butter has melted, add the onion and fry over a high heat for 3–4 minutes. Cover the pan with a lid, then reduce the heat and cook for 15 minutes until soft (see tip).

2 Add the garlic and mushrooms, turn up the heat and fry, uncovered, for a further 5 minutes. Tip in the crayfish tails and toss everything together.

3 Pour in the cream and boil over a high heat for about 2 minutes until reduced by half and thickened slightly. Add the Parmesan, lemon juice and herbs, season with salt and pepper and stir together until heated through and piping hot.

4 Griddle or toast the slices of bread, place on plates and spoon over the crayfish mixture. Serve immediately with a few salad leaves and lemon wedges.

## MARY'S FOOLPROOF TIP

After cooking the onion, this dish is very speedy to make and should be assembled quickly!

# MACKEREL PÂTÉ WITH LIME

This tasty pâté is so quick to prepare. It has a mousse-like texture but needs no gelatine to set it. Serve in individual ramekins or a large bowl.

---

Serves 4–6

PREPARE AHEAD
Can be made up to 2 days ahead and kept chilled in the fridge.

---

300g (11oz) smoked mackerel fillets, skinned (see tip)

1 x 250g tub of full-fat mascarpone cheese

1 tsp coarsely ground black pepper

finely grated zest and juice of 1 lime

a few sprigs of parsley

salt (optional)

griddled toast, to serve

1 Measure the mackerel and mascarpone into a food processor and whizz until fairly smooth. Tip into a bowl, then add the pepper, half the lime zest and all the juice. Stir to combine and then check the seasoning, adding salt if needed.

2 Spoon the mixture into a serving dish or individual little bowls, miniature jars or ramekins, scatter with the remaining lime zest and top with sprigs of parsley, then serve with griddled toast.

---

## MARY'S FOOLPROOF TIP

Smoked mackerel fillets come in packets in the pre-packed chiller section of the supermarket. They come with the skin on and it is easily removed by just peeling away from the flesh. Check there are no bones before mixing with the mascarpone.

---

# SMOKED HADDOCK AND EGG MOUSSE WITH CAPER VINAIGRETTE

These intense-flavoured little mousses make the perfect starter – their smoky, creamy taste is offset by the caper dressing and fresh green leaves.

Serves 8

PREPARE AHEAD
Can be made up to a day ahead and kept chilled in the fridge.

300g (11oz) undyed smoked haddock fillets

butter, for greasing

2 eggs

2 leaves (4g) of gelatine (see tip)

200ml (7fl oz) full-fat crème fraîche

100ml (3½fl oz) full-fat mayonnaise

2 tbsp lemon juice

2 tbsp finely chopped dill, plus extra sprigs to serve

2 tbsp drained capers, chopped

3 tbsp boiling water

salt and freshly ground black pepper

FOR THE CAPER VINAIGRETTE

1 tsp Dijon mustard

6 tbsp olive oil

2 tsp caster sugar

1 tbsp chopped capers with their brine

1 tbsp drained whole capers

TO SERVE

8 quail's eggs

salad leaves

brown bread

**1** Preheat the oven to 180°C/160°C fan/Gas 4. Line eight ramekins with cling film.

**2** Place the haddock on a sheet of buttered foil, season with a little salt and pepper (bearing in mind that smoked haddock can be quite salty) and wrap into a parcel. Put the foil-wrapped fish on a baking tray and bake in the oven for about 15 minutes or until cooked through, then set aside to cool.

**3** Bring a pan of water to the boil and boil the two hen's eggs for 10 minutes, then rinse under cold water, peel and roughly chop into small chunks. Boil the quail's eggs (for serving) in another pan for 1½ minutes, then drain and leave to cool in cold water before peeling and cutting in half.

**4** Soak the gelatine in cold water and leave for 5 minutes to become pliable.

**5** Measure the crème fraîche and mayonnaise into a bowl with the lemon juice, dill and capers. Add the chopped hen's eggs. Peel the skin from the haddock and flake it into the bowl. Season with salt and pepper and stir to combine.

**6** Measure the boiling water into a bowl. Squeeze all the water from the soaked gelatine, add it to the bowl, and stir to dissolve completely. After 2 minutes, add to the fish mixture and mix in gently but thoroughly. Spoon into the lined ramekins and level the tops. Cover with cling film and set in the fridge for at least 3 hours.

**7** For the vinaigrette, whisk all the ingredients together and season to taste.

**8** To serve, turn each mousse out of its ramekin on to a plate and top with two quail's egg halves and a sprig of dill. Add some salad leaves, pour the caper vinaigrette around the mousse and serve with brown bread on the side.

## MARY'S FOOLPROOF TIP

Sheet gelatine can vary depending on the brand, so read the packet instructions before using. It's best to weigh the leaves before using as they can vary in size too.

# LOBSTER TAILS WITH TARRAGON AIOLI AND ASPARAGUS

**This dish may sound grand, and it looks very impressive on the plate, yet it is, in fact, very simple to prepare. Lobster tails are available, fresh or frozen, from fishmongers or large supermarkets.**

Serves 4

PREPARE AHEAD
Assemble up to 6 hours ahead and keep chilled in the fridge. Bring to room temperature before serving.

2 raw lobster tails

12 large asparagus spears, woody ends snapped off

salt and freshly ground black pepper

FOR THE TARRAGON AIOLI

6 tbsp full-fat mayonnaise

4 tbsp full-fat crème fraîche

1 garlic clove, crushed

1 tbsp lemon juice

1 tbsp finely chopped tarragon

TO SERVE

lamb's lettuce

4 lemon wedges

1 First cook the lobster tails. Bring a saucepan of salted water to the boil and add the lobster tails. Bring back up to the boil and cook for about 5 minutes or until the flesh is firm and the shells are bright pink (see tip). Drain and set aside to cool.

2 When cold, use a large kitchen knife to cut each tail in half lengthways, slicing through the flesh and the shell. Using your fingers, carefully loosen the meat from each shell half, keeping it in one piece. Turn each piece of meat over and place in the opposite shell half so that the prettier side is now facing up.

3 Cook the asparagus spears in a large pan of boiling salted water for 3–4 minutes or until just tender. Drain and refresh in a large bowl of cold water, then drain again and pat dry.

4 To make the aioli, mix all the ingredients together in a bowl and season with salt and pepper to taste.

5 To assemble, arrange some lamb's lettuce on four individual plates and add a wedge of lemon to each plate. Spoon a dollop of aioli on the side or serve in a small dipping bowl. Arrange half a lobster tail next to this, with three asparagus spears on the other side, then sprinkle with black pepper to serve.

### MARY'S FOOLPROOF TIP

Don't overcook the lobster tails or they will become rubbery. Releasing the meat from the shell and turning it over makes it easier to eat as well as looking more decorative.

# CRAB QUENELLES WITH SAMPHIRE

Rather like fine asparagus in appearance, samphire is a fleshy, green-stemmed plant that grows by the sea and hence goes well with fish and seafood. You can buy it fresh from good fish counters in supermarkets or fishmongers, if you are lucky enough to have one nearby.

Serves 6

PREPARE AHEAD

Can be assembled up to 6 hours ahead and kept in the fridge. The crab mixture can be made up to a day ahead and kept covered in a bowl until required.

175g (6oz) fresh samphire

6 large tomatoes, deseeded and finely diced

6 sprigs of dill

FOR THE CRAB MIXTURE

100g (4oz) brown crabmeat

200g (7oz) white crabmeat

3 tbsp full-fat cream cheese

1 tbsp full-fat mayonnaise

1 tsp lemon juice

1 tsp Dijon mustard

1 tbsp chopped dill

salt and freshly ground black pepper

TO SERVE

French dressing (see page 186) or dressing of your choice

brown bread

1 First make the crab mixture. Measure all the ingredients into a bowl, season with pepper and a little salt and mix to combine.

2 Trim any woody ends off the samphire. Cook the samphire in boiling water (no need to add salt as the samphire is already salty) for 2 minutes until tender (see tip). Drain and refresh under cold water (see tip on page 184) before patting dry on kitchen paper.

3 Lay out six individual plates. Arrange the samphire on each plate then scatter the tomato pieces over the samphire.

4 Make a quenelle by scooping up a little of the crab mixture with one tablespoon and moulding it with another tablespoon into a clean-cut egg shape. Place this in the middle of the samphire, garnish with a sprig of dill and repeat with the remaining crab mixture to make six quenelles, each garnished with dill.

5 Drizzle a little French dressing around the samphire and serve with brown bread.

## MARY'S FOOLPROOF TIP

It is important not to overcook the samphire or it will be mushy – it needs to have a little bite to offset the soft crab.

# OLD-FASHIONED HAM HOCK TERRINE

**This tasty and colourful terrine is ideal for serving a crowd – great for a picnic or buffet table as well as a dinner-party starter. It's delicious served with piccalilli or Dijon mustard and crusty bread.**

Serves 10–12

**PREPARE AHEAD**
Can be made 3–5 days ahead.

2 x 1kg (2lb 3oz) ham hocks

1 carrot, peeled and chopped

2–3 celery sticks, chopped

1 bunch of thyme

a few black peppercorns

2 small onions, sliced

3 leaves (5g) of gelatine (see tip on page 53)

leaves of 1 bunch of parsley, chopped

1 tbsp yellow mustard seeds

**1** You will need a 900g (2lb) loaf tin. Preheat the oven to 160°C/140°C fan/Gas 3 and line the tin with cling film (see tip).

**2** Put the ham hocks into a deep, ovenproof saucepan. Add the carrot, celery, thyme, peppercorns and onions. Pour in enough cold water to just cover the hocks and then bring to the boil over a high heat. Skim off any fat, cover with a lid and transfer to the oven to cook for about 3 hours or until the meat is falling off the bone and completely tender.

**3** Transfer the cooked hocks to a large bowl and set aside to cool. Strain the ham cooking liquid through a sieve, then pour 1 litre (1¾ pints) into a large saucepan, and boil to reduce the liquid to 600ml (1 pint), skimming off any fat or scum that rises to the surface. Taste the stock and if it is too salty, remove some of it and top up with water. Pour into a clean pan.

**4** Soak the gelatine in cold water for 5 minutes. Reheat the 600ml (1 pint) of stock in the pan, then squeeze the water from the soaked gelatine and add the soft leaves to the cooking liquid, stirring until the gelatine has dissolved.

**5** Remove the fat and bone from the ham hocks and discard, then flake the meat into largish chunks. Sprinkle the parsley into the base of the prepared loaf tin and pour in a little of the gelatine liquid. Add a layer of ham pieces and scatter over a few mustard seeds, then add a little more liquid, followed by another layer of ham. Continue layering up in this way, adding more liquid and seeds between the layers. You may not need all the liquid – just enough to reach the top.

**6** Cover with cling film and chill overnight in the fridge until set and firm (do not press with weights). Turn out, then cut the terrine into thick slices while still chilled and allow it to sit at room temperature for a few minutes before serving.

## MARY'S FOOLPROOF TIP

Before lining your tin, rinse it with a little cold water first. Shake out the excess but don't dry it – the residual water helps the cling film to stick when you line the tin.

FISH

# SPICED, BLACKENED SALMON

**A simple but unusual way of cooking salmon – the cumin and ground coriander sear the crust to give a blackened appearance and a mildly spicy flavour that's lifted by the lime and fresh coriander in the yoghurt sauce. The salmon is also great eaten cold as a salad the next day.**

Serves 6

## PREPARE AHEAD
The salmon can be marinated up to 8 hours ahead and the yoghurt sauce made up to 3 days ahead. Once cooked, the fish can be kept chilled in the fridge until the next day to eat cold.

6 x 150g (5oz) middle-cut salmon fillets, skinned

4 tbsp olive oil

1 tbsp ground cumin

1 tbsp ground coriander

salt and freshly ground black pepper

### FOR THE SAUCE

3 tbsp natural Greek yoghurt

1 tbsp chopped coriander

finely grated zest of 1 lime

salad leaves, to serve

1 Arrange the salmon fillets in a dish, pour over 3 tablespoons of the olive oil, sprinkle with the spices, season with salt and pepper and toss to coat. Cover and transfer to the fridge to marinate for 30 minutes.

2 Pour the remaining oil into a large frying pan over a high heat, add the marinated salmon fillets and fry for a minute on each side to seal. Reduce the heat to medium and fry for a further 4–5 minutes on each side until blackened and just cooked through (see tip).

3 To make the sauce, mix the yoghurt with the coriander and lime zest and season with salt and pepper.

4 Serve the salmon with salad leaves and a dollop of the yoghurt sauce on top.

## MARY'S FOOLPROOF TIPS

Middle-cut fillets are taken from the middle of the salmon, ensuring that they are the same shape and thickness, so will cook at the same rate.

Don't overcook the salmon and take care when turning over the fillets. If they are sticking, leave for another minute – it means the flesh is not sealed.

# SALMON AND HERB COULIBIAC

The crisp filo pastry and flavoursome rice make this coulibiac lighter than the classic version of this traditional Russian fish in pastry dish. Great for a party, as it serves a good number of people, this is best served hot.

Serves 8

**PREPARE AHEAD**
Can be assembled up to 6 hours ahead and cooked to serve. Keep chilled in the fridge but bring to room temperature just before cooking, or cook slightly longer to ensure the filling is heated through.

500g (1lb 2oz) salmon fillet, skinned

175g (6oz) long-grain rice

75g (3oz) butter, plus extra for greasing

2 onions, roughly chopped

2 garlic cloves, crushed

1 small fresh red chilli, deseeded and diced

200g (7oz) button mushrooms, sliced

finely grated zest and juice of ½ large lemon

2 tbsp chopped parsley

1 tbsp snipped chives

6 sheets (each 25 x 45cm/10 x 18in) of filo pastry

salt and freshly ground black pepper

watercress sprigs, to serve (optional)

FOR THE SAUCE

300g (11oz) natural Greek yoghurt

1 small bunch of parsley, chopped

1 tbsp snipped chives

juice of ½ large lemon

1 Butter a large sheet of foil and sit the salmon on top, then season with salt and pepper and wrap in the foil to make a parcel. Place the foil parcel on a baking tray and bake in the oven for 15–20 minutes until cooked through. Set aside to cool.

2 Meanwhile, cook the rice until tender in salted boiling water according to the packet instructions, then drain and tip into a bowl.

3 Melt 25g (1oz) of the butter in a large frying pan over a medium heat, add the onions and fry for 3 minutes, with a lid on the pan, until starting to soften. Add the garlic and chilli and fry for 30 seconds, then add the mushrooms and fry for another 3 minutes.

4 Stir in the cooked rice and remove from the heat before adding the lemon zest and juice with the parsley and chives. Break the cooked salmon into large pieces and add to the rice, season with salt and pepper and carefully stir to combine. Set aside to cool and then chill in the fridge for 30 minutes. While the mixture is chilling, preheat the oven to 200°C/180°C fan/Gas 6.

5 Melt the remaining butter in a small pan. Lay two sheets of filo pastry lengthways and side by side on a piece of baking paper – they should overlap slightly (by about 5cm/2in). Brush with the melted butter and seal along the middle to make a 45cm (18in) square. Lay two more filo sheets side by side on top, at right angles to the first layer, and brush with butter. Lay the last two sheets over the top, in the same direction as the first two sheets, and brush with butter to make three layers forming a 45cm (18in) square. (See also tips overleaf.)

*Continues overleaf*

# SALMON AND HERB COULIBIAC *Continued*

**6** Arrange the salmon and rice filling along one-third of the square in a long log shape, leaving a gap of at least 5cm (2in) from the edge of the pastry. Fold in the sides and then tightly roll up the pastry around the filling to create a strudel shape about 30cm (12in) long. Use the baking paper to help to roll it up firmly. Make sure the ends of the pastry are sealed and then transfer the parcel with the paper to a baking sheet.

**7** Brush more melted butter over the top and then bake in the oven for 30–35 minutes or until the pastry is crisp and golden brown.

**8** For the sauce, add all the ingredients to a bowl, season with salt and pepper and stir to combine. Slice the cooked coulibiac and serve with sprigs of watercress (if using) and the sauce.

......................................................................................................

## MARY'S FOOLPROOF TIPS

It is important for the filo to remain soft while you're handling it, so keep it covered with a clean, damp tea towel if working in a hot kitchen.

Placing the second pastry layer at right angles to the first and last layers forms a lattice that will strengthen the sheets by helping them hold together.

Make sure your pastry square is no smaller than 45cm (18in); it needs to be large enough to wrap around the filling to ensure the coulibiac doesn't split when cooked.

......................................................................................................

# SMOKED HADDOCK
# AND SWEETCORN CHOWDER

**Filled with chunks of smoked haddock and tender potato, this sustaining, creamy chowder is much more than just a soup – an all-in-one, hearty dish to warm you up on a chilly day.**

Serves 6

PREPARE AHEAD
Can be made up to a day ahead and stored in the fridge overnight.

50g (2oz) butter

1 small leek,
 finely sliced

450g (1lb) potatoes,
 peeled and cut into
 2cm (¾ in) chunks

40g (1½oz) plain flour

600ml (1 pint) fish or
 vegetable stock

1 x 198g tin of
 sweetcorn, drained

700g (1½lb) smoked
 haddock fillets,
 skinned and chopped
 into bite-sized pieces

600ml (1 pint)
 full-fat milk (see tip)

salt and freshly ground
 black pepper

chopped dill, to garnish

1 Melt the butter in a large pan. Add the leek, stirring to coat in the butter, then cover with a lid and cook gently over a low heat for about 10 minutes until beginning to soften. Add the potatoes and cook for a further 1–2 minutes.

2 Stir in the flour and then add the stock, pouring it in gradually and stirring until smooth. Season with pepper to taste, adding no salt at this stage as the fish can be very salty. Bring the mixture to the boil and simmer for 10–15 minutes until the potatoes are tender.

3 Add the sweetcorn to the pan with the smoked haddock and milk, then bring back up to the boil and simmer gently for a further 5–10 minutes (see tip) until the fish is cooked.

4 Adjust the seasoning, adding salt and pepper to taste, and garnish with dill to serve.

## MARY'S FOOLPROOF TIPS

If you have no full-fat milk, just add a little cream to semi-skimmed milk.

Be gentle with the chowder – no fast boiling or rapid mixing; you want all the flavours to infuse but without breaking up the fish and potatoes.

# SALMON FILLETS WITH HERBS AND RED PEPPER

Perfect for preparing ahead, these salmon pieces with their decorative topping of herby cream cheese and roasted red peppers would be impressive to serve at a smart dinner party. Choose fillets cut from the middle of the fish to ensure they are all the same size and shape and cook at the same rate.

Serves 6

PREPARE AHEAD
Can be assembled up to 12 hours ahead.

280g (10oz) full-fat cream cheese

30g (1oz) Parmesan cheese, finely grated

1 garlic clove, crushed

2 tbsp finely snipped chives

6 x 125g (4½oz) salmon fillets, skinned

finely grated zest and juice of 1 large lemon

1 small bunch of parsley, finely chopped

150g (5oz) roasted red peppers from a jar, drained and very thinly sliced

salt and freshly ground black pepper

1 Preheat the oven 200°C/180°C fan/Gas 6 and line a baking tray with baking paper.

2 Add the cream cheese to a bowl with the Parmesan, garlic and chives. Season with salt and pepper and stir together. Season the salmon with salt and pepper and spread the cream cheese mixture equally over each fillet.

3 Mix the lemon zest and parsley together and sprinkle over each fillet, pressing down lightly. Place the fillets on the prepared baking tray (see tip) and arrange the peppers on top in a pretty pattern.

4 Roast in the oven for 15–18 minutes or until the salmon is cooked through. Squeeze over the lemon juice and serve hot with new potatoes and dressed salad leaves.

## MARY'S FOOLPROOF TIP

Place the salmon fillets fairly close to each other on the baking tray so that they keep each other moist and don't dry out during cooking. You will know when they are cooked, as the flesh will become a matt pink colour all the way through.

# FOOLPROOF FISH

Fish forms an important part of a healthy, balanced diet, providing a good source of protein, a variety of vitamins and minerals and some essential fatty acids. It is also a wonderful alternative to meat, offering a lighter choice for every day and an enjoyable way to add variety to your weekly diet. I like to include it in more luxurious and indulgent dishes, too. There are few things better than a comforting fish pie (see page 80) on a cold winter's day, for instance, or a show-stopping salmon coulibiac (see page 65) to wow your guests at a dinner party. But however you like to serve fish – whether for a light and virtuous weekday supper or a special-occasion treat – it is well worth learning how best to prepare, handle and cook it so that you can appreciate its delicate texture and flavour.

MAIN TYPES

Fish can be divided into three main categories:

*White fish* Low in fat and delicate in texture and flavour, these include cod, sea bass, plaice and sole.

*Oily fish* As well as being extremely flavoursome, these are a brilliant source of omega-3 fatty acids. This category includes mackerel, salmon and sardines.

*Shellfish* These include lobster, crayfish, prawns, crab and mussels.

CHOOSING AND PREPARING FISH

DO . . .

*Check for freshness* The skin and eyes (for a whole fish) should be bright, the flesh firm and moist. It shouldn't smell fishy or unpleasant. Shellfish should be undamaged; prawns and scallops should be plump and firm with a sweet rather than fishy smell. Any mussels that are open when raw should close when firmly tapped; they should be discarded if they don't.

*Buy sustainably caught or farmed fish* Most fishmongers and large supermarkets sell only fish from sustainable sources, but if you are unsure check the packaging for an ecolabel from MSC (Marine Stewardship Council) or FOS (Friends of the Sea).

*Keep fish cool* Store in the coldest part of the fridge.

*Get help with preparation* If you're new to cooking it, ask your fishmonger to scale, gut, fillet and pin-bone your fish for you, as this can be time-consuming and requires a little experience.

*Cook fish as soon as you can after buying* Fish should be eaten as fresh as possible.

DON'T . . .

*Freeze fish for an extended period of time* Use white fish within 3 months and oily fish within 2 months. Freezing fish for longer than this will affect its texture and flavour. Make sure it is well wrapped and labelled before freezing.

*Stand mussels in water* Clean mussels in an empty sink under a cold running tap. Don't allow them to sit in water as this will kill them. Place in a colander, cover with a damp tea towel and store in the fridge until ready to cook.

COOKING METHODS

As with meat, the key thing to remember when cooking fish is timing. It is easy to overcook it, but if you follow these simple guidelines, you should be able to serve perfectly cooked, succulent and tender fish.

ROASTING AND GRILLING

These methods are best for quickly cooking whole fish or large fillets of fish.

DO . . .

*Roast in a hot oven* at about 200°C/180°C fan/Gas 6. The timings will vary depending on the type of fish – check the packaging or with your fishmonger.

*Preheat the oven or grill* at least 10 minutes before use to ensure it has reached the correct temperature.

*Score the flesh* when grilling whole fish. This helps the fish cook more evenly and allows any added flavourings to permeate the meat. Cut 3–4 diagonal slits into the flesh, no more than 1cm (½in) deep.

*Use a fish slice to turn fish* Fish is very delicate when cooked, so take care when turning it halfway through grilling.

PAN-FRYING AND GRIDDLING

Cooking fish over a direct heat in a frying or griddle pan is the quickest way to cook it. It is often used to cook leaner, meatier varieties, such as tuna steaks, prawns or sea bass fillets. Fishcakes and breaded fillets can also be pan-fried, but they require longer cooking over a medium heat rather than quick cooking at a high temperature.

DO . . .

*Use a little fat* Lean fish needs some fat to prevent it sticking to the pan. Lightly rub a little oil all over the fillet or steak to coat it before cooking.

*Ensure the pan is piping hot* The fish should sizzle on being added to the pan; it needs to cook at the highest temperature possible to ensure that it cooks quickly and doesn't dry out.

*Guarantee crispy skin* If you are intending to eat the skin of the fish – that of a fillet of sea bass or bream, for example – place the fillet skin side down in the pan, cook over a high heat until golden and crispy and then carefully flip over to finish cooking.

DON'T . . .

*Move the fish fillet or steak around during cooking* Place the fish in the pan and leave it to fry, without moving it, until it's time to turn it over to cook the other side. The texture of fish is very delicate and too much movement could cause it to fall apart.

## POACHING

Poaching is the method most often used when making a fish curry or soup, when large chunks of fish are added to a simmering broth or sauce. It is also possible to poach a whole fish, such as salmon, which can make a wonderful centrepiece for a buffet.

DO . . .

*Use large, even-sized chunks of fish* If they are too small, they will break up easily when cooked.

*Choose firm, meaty varieties for soups, stews and curries* Monkfish or cod loin are good options here as they have a firm-textured flesh that keeps its shape when cooked; they are less likely to disintegrate during poaching.

*Simmer gently* If the sauce or broth is boiling too vigorously, it will cause the fish to overcook and fall apart.

*Cover the pan with a lid* This keeps the steam circulating inside the pan so that the fish cooks evenly and stays moist and tender.

## EN PAPILLOTE

One of my favourite ways to cook fish is 'en papillote' – that is, wrapped up in a parcel of baking paper or foil with some aromatic ingredients for flavouring such as lemon, dill, fennel, or finely chopped celery or onions. The parcel is baked in the oven, but the fish cooks in the steam that is created from its own juices inside the parcel. This is a great way to keep fish moist and cleverly creates a very tasty dish by concentrating all the flavours in one place. Ensure the parcel is tightly sealed to prevent any juices or steam from escaping.

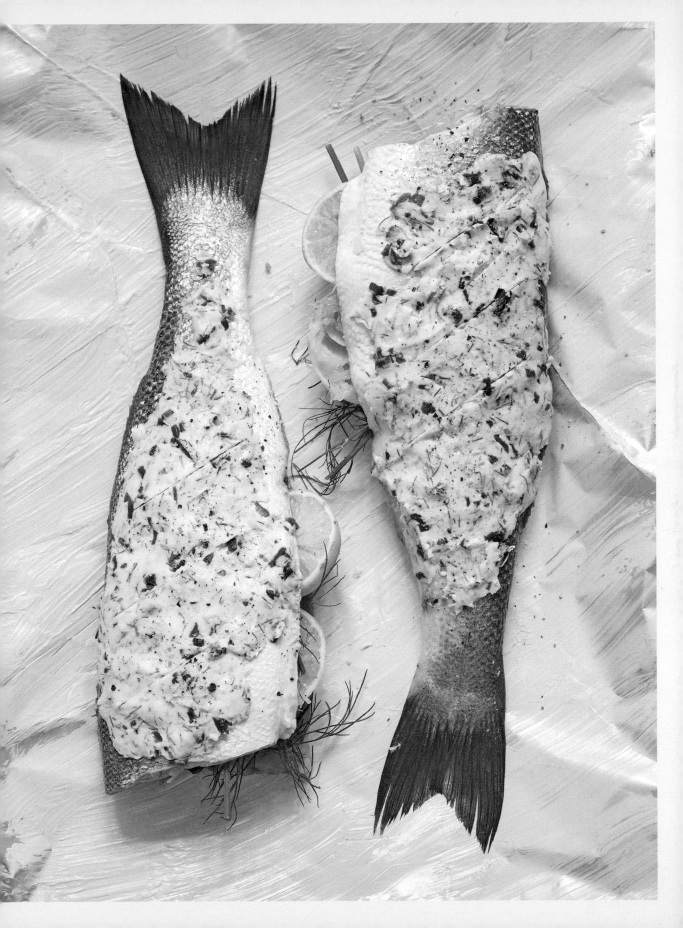

# MONKFISH FILLETS WITH MUSHROOM AND BACON SAUCE

**Perfect for a dinner party with its rich and tasty sauce, this is monkfish at its finest. Serve with tenderstem broccoli and rice or baby new potatoes.**

Serves 6

6 x 150g (5oz) monkfish fillets, skinned and trimmed (see tip)

3 tbsp plain flour

2 tbsp oil

a knob of butter

6 rashers of smoked, streaky bacon, chopped into small pieces

1 small onion, finely chopped

200g (7oz) button mushrooms, halved

200ml (7fl oz) full-fat crème fraîche

juice of ½ lemon

1 tsp Dijon mustard

3 tbsp chopped parsley

salt and freshly ground black pepper

1 Preheat the oven to 200°C/180°C fan/Gas 6 and line a baking tray with baking paper.

2 Season the monkfish fillets with salt and pepper. Sprinkle the flour on to a plate and dust the fish until fully coated, shaking off any excess flour.

3 Place a frying pan over a high heat, add the oil and butter, and when the butter is foaming, add the fillets and fry for 2–3 minutes until the fish is sealed and lightly golden, turning once. Transfer to the prepared baking tray and pour over any buttery juices from the pan. Roast in the oven for 8–10 minutes until still firm and the flesh has turned white and is cooked through.

4 Meanwhile, wipe the frying pan (to remove any traces of flour so they don't catch) and add the bacon. Fry over a high heat until crisp and then transfer to a plate. Tip in the onion and fry for 3 minutes, then cover, reduce the heat to medium and cook for a further 5 minutes until soft. Remove the lid, turn up the heat, add the mushrooms and fry for a few minutes, stirring constantly, until golden.

5 Add the crème fraîche, lemon juice and mustard with half the cooked bacon and half the chopped parsley. Bring to the boil and allow to boil for a few minutes until the sauce is reduced and thickened slightly, then season to taste with salt and pepper.

6 Slice each of the fillets into three and arrange on a plate, spoon over the sauce and garnish with the reserved bacon and parsley.

## MARY'S FOOLPROOF TIP

Make sure the skin and thin membrane have been removed from the fillets. The membrane can tighten during cooking and restrict the fillets in the pan. Sprinkle a bit of salt on your fingers to help to grip the membrane, which can be slimy, and pull it off.

# WHOLE SEA BASS WITH LIME AND DILL BUTTER

**Tender sea bass wrapped in foil and cooked either in the oven or on a barbecue. Lime and dill sharpen the flavour of the delicate fish. Piquanté peppers are sweet-tasting baby bell peppers that you can buy pickled in jars, either mild or hot – I've used the mild variety here.**

Serves 4

PREPARE AHEAD
The sauce can be made in advance and stored in the fridge for up to 2 days.
The fish can be prepared and kept chilled in its foil wrapper for up to 6 hours
in advance; cook and serve immediately.

100g (4oz) butter, softened, plus extra for greasing

finely grated zest and juice of 2 limes (reserving the squeezed lime halves)

4 mild picanté peppers from a jar, drained and finely chopped

6 sprigs of dill, leaves chopped (reserving the stalks), plus extra chopped dill to garnish

2 x 700g (1½lb) whole sea bass, each gutted and fins and head removed (see tip)

200ml (7fl oz) full-fat crème fraîche

2 tsp Dijon mustard

1 tsp caster sugar

salt and freshly ground black pepper

1 Preheat the oven to 200°C/180°C fan/Gas 6 and grease two large sheets of foil with butter.

2 To make the lime butter, measure the softened butter into a bowl and add half of each of the lime zest and juice and of the chopped peppers and dill. Season with salt and pepper and mix well until combined.

3 Using a sharp knife, make three slashes along each side of the sea bass, and rub as much butter as possible into the slashes and over the skin of the fish. Use the dill stalks and squeezed lime halves to fill the cavity of each fish. Place a stuffed sea bass on top of each piece of foil, wrapping the foil around and crimping the edges to make a watertight parcel (see tip). Cook in the oven – or on a hot barbecue – for about 20 minutes, turning halfway through.

4 To make the sauce, place the crème fraîche in a bowl with the mustard, sugar and the remaining lime zest and juice and chopped peppers and dill. Mix together and taste for seasoning – adding salt and pepper and a little more sugar, if you like.

5 Remove the foil from the cooked sea bass, sprinkle with extra dill and serve with the sauce. To serve at the table, lift the fillets from each side of the spine, or flake the fish, and allow everyone to help themselves.

## MARY'S FOOLPROOF TIPS

You can always ask a fishmonger to prepare the fish for you.

The foil must be sealed around the fish or the butter will drip out. When cooking, slide directly on to the oven shelf; if on a baking sheet, the skin can tend to stick.

# ALL-IN-ONE FISH GRATIN

**This tasty, warming dish would be ideal for a weekday supper for the family. Serve hot with peas or a green salad.**

Serves 6

PREPARE AHEAD
Can be assembled up to 8 hours ahead – allow the sauce to cool before mixing in the fish.

FREEZE
Freezes well raw – provided the fish hasn't been previously frozen and defrosted.

750g (1lb 10oz) medium potatoes

3 eggs

75g (3oz) butter

1 onion, chopped

200g (7oz) button mushrooms, sliced

50g (2oz) plain flour

450ml (15fl oz) hot milk

100ml (3½fl oz) white wine

1 tsp Dijon mustard

75g (3oz) mature Cheddar cheese, grated

1 tbsp snipped chives

750g (1lb 10oz) mixed fish fillets (such as cod and smoked haddock), skinned and sliced into pieces

salt and freshly ground black pepper

1 You will need a 1.75-litre (3-pint) ovenproof dish. Preheat the oven to 200°C/180°C fan/Gas 6.

2 Peel and slice each potato into 2–3 large, even-sized pieces. Place in a pan of salted water, bring to the boil and cook for 8–10 minutes until just tender (see tip) but not falling apart. Drain and refresh under cold water, then leave to cool.

3 Meanwhile, put the eggs into a pan of cold water. Bring to the boil and boil for 8 minutes, then drain, run under cold water, then peel and slice into quarters.

4 Melt 50g (2oz) of the butter in a deep frying pan over a high heat, add the onion and fry for 5 minutes until soft. Add the mushrooms and fry for a further 2 minutes, then season with salt and pepper.

5 Sprinkle in the flour and then blend in the milk, stirring constantly. Keep stirring until smooth and thickened, then add the wine. Add the mustard and season well with salt and pepper. Tip in 50g (2oz) of the grated cheese with the chives and stir to mix. The sauce will be thick.

6 Add the fish to the sauce and spoon into the ovenproof dish, then add the hard-boiled egg quarters, pushing them down so they're submerged in the sauce.

7 Slice the cooled potatoes into even-sized discs, then arrange on top of the fish mixture. Melt the remaining butter and drizzle over the potatoes before sprinkling with the remaining cheese.

8 Bake in the oven for 50–60 minutes until golden and bubbling. Leave to stand for 5–10 minutes before serving.

## MARY'S FOOLPROOF TIP

Ensure the potatoes are nearly cooked (no longer firm) before arranging on top.

# POULTRY
# & GAME

# SPICED CHICKEN SKEWERS WITH TZATZIKI

These tasty skewers are great for serving a crowd – you could cook them on a barbecue if you prefer.
The za'atar I've used in the marinade for the chicken is a Middle Eastern spice mix made up of thyme,
sumac and sesame seeds. It's readily available in supermarkets.

Makes 8 skewers

PREPARE AHEAD
The skewers can be assembled up to a day ahead, ready to fry. Make the dip
(without the cucumber) up to a day ahead, adding the cucumber no more than
2 hours before serving.

2 x 150g (5oz)
  skinless and boneless
  chicken breasts
2 tbsp oil
2 tsp ground cumin
2 tsp ground coriander
2 tsp za'atar
  spice blend
finely grated zest
  of 1 lemon
salt and freshly ground
  black pepper

FOR THE TZATZIKI
200g (7oz)
  natural yoghurt
½ cucumber, peeled,
  deseeded and cut
  into small pieces
2 tbsp chopped mint,
  plus extra, to garnish
2 tbsp chopped dill,
  plus extra, to garnish
1 tbsp lemon juice

1 You will need eight metal or wooden skewers (see tip) and a frying pan wide
enough to accommodate these.

2 Cut the chicken breasts into long thin strips. Tip into a bowl, add half the
oil and toss together. Scatter in the spices and lemon zest, season with salt and
pepper and toss again until coated. Cover and leave to marinate in the fridge for
a minimum of 1 hour or overnight (see tip).

3 To make the tzatziki, mix all the ingredients together in a bowl, season with salt
and pepper and stir to combine.

4 Thread the chicken strips on to the skewers so the meat is entwined around
each skewer – you will need 2–3 pieces per skewer.

5 Pour the remaining oil into your frying pan and set over a high heat. Add the
skewers – cooking them in two batches, if needed – and fry for 2–3 minutes on
each side until dark golden and cooked through. Serve hot with the tzatziki.

## MARY'S FOOLPROOF TIPS

If using wooden skewers, soak in water for 30 minutes before using – this prevents
them from burning.

Marinating the chicken enhances the flavour and keeps the meat tender.

# SMOKED TEXAN CHICKEN WINGS

**Great for a barbecue or picnic, these have a hint of chilli but are warmly smoky rather than flaming firecracker. Chicken wings consisting of just the wing joint without the tip are best for this dish. Bear in mind that you'll need to marinate them for at least 2 hours before cooking.**

Serves 6

PREPARE AHEAD
Can be left to marinate up to a day ahead.

FREEZE
Once marinated, the chicken wings can be frozen, then defrosted to roast.

1kg (2lb 3oz) chicken wings (tips removed)

1 tbsp light muscovado sugar

1 tbsp tomato ketchup

2 tsp sweet smoked paprika (see tip on page 143)

1 garlic clove, crushed

1 fresh red chilli, deseeded and finely chopped

2 tbsp Worcestershire sauce

2 tbsp olive oil

salt and freshly ground black pepper

1 Place the chicken wings in a large bowl and season with salt and pepper. Measure the remaining ingredients into another bowl and mix to combine.

2 Pour the mixture over the chicken wings, tossing to coat, then cover with cling film and leave to marinate in the fridge for a minimum of 2 hours or overnight (see tip).

3 When you are ready to cook the chicken, preheat the oven to 220°C/200°C fan/Gas 7 or heat up the barbecue.

4 Transfer the chicken wings and marinade to a roasting tin, arrange in a single layer and roast for about 30 minutes, turning once halfway through, until cooked through and deep golden in colour.

5 Serve hot or cold with salad and coleslaw (see page 209).

## MARY'S FOOLPROOF TIP

Marinating the chicken wings gives depth of flavour and prevents them from drying out. You could use a resealable freezer bag instead of a bowl, if you prefer.

# CHICKEN AND BACON LATTICE PIE

This pie with its lattice topping would make a wonderful centrepiece for a family meal or other gathering. My granddaughters Abby and Grace helped me to make it for the TV programme. Using bought puff pastry is much easier and quicker than making your own, and if time is very short you can just cover it with pastry rather than making the lattice – though it won't be nearly so impressive!

Serves 6

PREPARE AHEAD
Can be made up to 2 days ahead.

FREEZE
Freezes well uncooked.

6 chicken legs (thigh and drumstick), skin removed

4 celery sticks, cut into small dice

4 bay leaves, roughly sliced

200ml (7fl oz) white wine

300ml (10fl oz) chicken stock

250g (9oz) smoked back bacon (about 7 rashers), cut into small pieces

1 large onion, roughly chopped

50g (2oz) butter

60g (2½oz) plain flour, plus extra for dusting

2 tbsp full-fat crème fraîche

1 tbsp grainy mustard

2 x 375g packets of ready-rolled, all-butter puff pastry

1 egg, beaten

salt and freshly ground black pepper

1 You will need a 1.75-litre (3-pint) shallow, wide-based ovenproof dish, about 25cm (10in) in diameter. Preheat the oven to 160°C/140°C fan/Gas 3.

2 Put the chicken legs, celery and bay leaves into a large ovenproof saucepan, pour over the wine and stock and season with salt and pepper. Bring to the boil on a medium-high heat, cover with a lid and transfer to the oven to bake for 30–40 minutes or until the chicken legs are cooked and tender. Set aside to cool.

3 Once cool, remove the meat from the chicken bones. The bones can be reserved and used for a stock. Break the meat into bite-sized pieces before transferring to a bowl. Strain the stock, reserving the celery and discarding the bay leaves, and measure out the liquid. You should have about 750ml (1 pint 6fl oz); if not, make up to this amount with a little extra stock or white wine.

4 Heat a large frying pan and fry the bacon pieces on a medium-high heat for 3 minutes. Add the onion, cover with a lid and fry for a further 10 minutes until the onion is softened. Add the butter, stir until melted, then sprinkle in the flour to make a roux. Pour the reserved liquid into the roux a little at a time, whisking as you add, and stir over a high heat until thickened to a smooth sauce consistency.

5 Season with salt and pepper, add the reserved celery with the crème fraîche and mustard, mix to combine and then stir in the chicken pieces. Spoon the filling into the ovenproof dish and level the top. Leave to cool and then chill in the fridge for 30 minutes.

*Continues overleaf*

# CHICKEN AND BACON LATTICE PIE *Continued*

**6** Meanwhile, prepare the pastry for the pie. On a lightly floured work surface, roll out each of the pastry sheets to about 3mm (⅛in) thick. Cut each piece into long, thick ribbons (about 3cm/1¼in wide) – you will need to make enough to cover the top of the dish (about 16 in total). Weave the ribbons together on a piece of baking paper (see tips), like a basket (see opposite), until you have a pastry top that is large enough to cover your pie. Chill in the fridge for 15 minutes to firm up – or even better, if time allows, freeze until solid.

**7** Take the filling out of the fridge and brush the edges of the dish with a little beaten egg. Carefully slide the pastry lattice from the paper and lay on top of the chilled filling. Trim the excess pastry around the rim and press to seal.

**8** Increase the oven temperature to 200°C/180°C fan/Gas 6. Brush the pastry with more beaten egg and bake for 30 minutes until the pastry is golden and cooked through, and the chicken is bubbling. Serve hot.

### MARY'S FOOLPROOF TIPS

To make the lattice topping, first draw a circle on a piece of baking paper, 5cm (2in) wider in diameter than your dish. It is so much easier to make the lattice on a piece of paper and then slide it on top of the dish.

Keep the lattice as tight as possible, and make sure that the pie lid is sealed firmly with egg wash, so that no filling escapes.

# CHICKEN CORDON BLEU

**For this version of the classic dish of chicken breasts stuffed with ham and cheese, I've used a coating of panko breadcrumbs as they stay so crisp and give a wonderful golden coating. Just fry them in a pan on the hob – no deep-fat fryer needed.**

Serves 6

PREPARE AHEAD
Can be assembled up to a day ahead. Place in a dish lined with baking paper and keep covered in the fridge until ready to fry.

FREEZE
Once assembled, these freeze well. Defrost thoroughly before cooking to serve.

6 equal-sized skinless and boneless chicken breasts

1 tbsp Dijon mustard

6 slices of good-quality ham

6 slices of Gruyère cheese

3 heaped tbsp plain flour

2 eggs, beaten

100g (4oz) panko breadcrumbs

1 tbsp paprika

4–6 tbsp oil

salt and freshly ground black pepper

**1** Slice through each chicken breast horizontally, leaving it attached along one side. Open out each breast like a book and lay it between two pieces of cling film. Use a rolling pin to bash each piece of chicken to about 5mm (¼in) thick (see tip on page 95).

**2** Remove the cling film and using a pastry brush, brush the inside of each breast with mustard and season with salt and pepper. Lay a slice of ham and a slice of cheese on one side of each breast. Fold over the chicken to its original shape, making sure none of the filling is hanging out, and season with salt and pepper.

**3** Take three bowls or plates: tip the flour into one and season with salt and pepper; pour the beaten eggs into another; and add the panko breadcrumbs and paprika to the third, mixing the spice and breadcrumbs together. Dip each stuffed chicken breast into the flour, then the egg and then the spiced breadcrumbs, and transfer to a large plate. Each breast should be well and evenly coated.

**4** Heat 2 tablespoons of the oil in a large frying pan over a medium-high heat. Pan-fry the chicken, two breasts at a time, for 8–10 minutes on each side, turning once, until golden all over and cooked through (see tip). If the breadcrumbs brown too quickly, turn the heat down a little. Once cooked, remove from the pan and keep warm in a low oven. Repeat for the remaining chicken breasts, adding a little more oil to the pan each time if needed.

**5** Serve the cooked chicken with a tomato and rocket salad.

## MARY'S FOOLPROOF TIP

You can check the chicken is cooked properly by taking a small sharp knife and making a small incision in the top of the breast. The chicken flesh should be white, not pink, on either side of the ham and cheese filling.

# CHICKEN SCHNITZEL WITH FRIED EGG

**Tender chicken breasts in golden breadcrumbs, each served with a fried egg
on top – perfect for a satisfying family supper.**

Serves 4

PREPARE AHEAD
The chicken pieces can be coated
up to 8 hours ahead, then fried with
the eggs to serve.

FREEZE
Once coated, the uncooked chicken
can be frozen.

4 small skinless and
  boneless chicken
  breasts (125–150g/
  4½–5oz each)

25g (1oz) plain flour

1 tsp mustard powder

1 egg, beaten

25g (1oz) panko
  breadcrumbs

a little paprika,
  for sprinkling

sunflower oil, for frying

4 eggs

salt and freshly ground
  black pepper

1 Place the chicken breasts on a board, cover with cling film and, using a rolling
pin, bash each piece of chicken to about 2cm (¾in) thick (see tip). Season the
breasts with salt and pepper.

2 Take three bowls or plates: tip the flour and mustard powder into one, combine
and season with salt and pepper; pour the beaten egg into another; and add the
panko breadcrumbs to the third. Dip each chicken breast into the seasoned flour,
then the egg and then the breadcrumbs. Sprinkle with paprika and transfer to a
large plate.

3 Pour a little sunflower oil into a large frying pan over a medium-high heat and
fry the chicken for 4–5 minutes on each side until golden and cooked through.
You may need to do this in two batches.

4 Transfer to a clean plate and cover in foil to keep warm. Wipe out the pan,
add a little more oil and fry the eggs over a medium heat for 2–3 minutes so the
whites are set and the yolks are still runny. Season the yolks with salt and pepper,
then serve each schnitzel with a fried egg on top.

## MARY'S FOOLPROOF TIP

Each chicken breast needs to be bashed to the same thickness as the other pieces
or they will cook at different rates.

# STUFFED CHICKEN THIGHS WITH LEMON SAUCE

**This is a great recipe for all the family – one that everyone will love. The honey drizzled over just before roasting gives the bacon-wrapped chicken thighs a lovely sheen. New potatoes and runner beans, or a simple green salad, make a perfect accompaniment.**

Serves 4–6

PREPARE AHEAD
Prepare the thighs up to a day ahead and then cook with the sauce to serve.

FREEZE
The chicken freezes well uncooked.

350g (12oz) pork sausage meat

4 tbsp chopped parsley

2 tsp chopped thyme leaves

grated zest of ½ large lemon

50g (2oz) Parmesan cheese, grated

8 skinless and boneless chicken thighs

8 rashers of smoked streaky bacon

2 tsp runny honey

salt and freshly ground black pepper

FOR THE
LEMON SAUCE

50g (2oz) butter

1 onion, finely chopped

40g (1½oz) plain flour

450ml (15fl oz) hot chicken stock

4 tbsp double cream

juice of ½ large lemon

1 tbsp chopped parsley

1 Preheat the oven to 200°C/180°C fan/Gas 6 and line a roasting tin with baking paper.

2 Put the sausage meat into a bowl, add the herbs, lemon zest and Parmesan, season with salt and pepper and mix well to combine. Shape into eight short sausages (no longer than the chicken thighs).

3 Place the chicken thighs, skinned side down, on a plate or board and open them out. Season with salt and pepper, then place a sausage in the centre of each thigh (where the bone was) and fold the chicken around it.

4 Using the flat of a large knife, stretch the bacon rashers out on a board and wrap around the chicken thighs – one rasher per thigh with the seam under the chicken.

5 Arrange the bacon-wrapped chicken thighs in the lined roasting tin, seam down, and drizzle over the honey. Roast in the oven for about 35 minutes or until cooked through, golden and crispy. Set aside to rest for 10 minutes.

6 While the chicken is roasting, make the lemon sauce. Melt the butter in a wide-based saucepan, add the onion and fry over a medium-high heat, stirring regularly, for about 10 minutes until soft and translucent. Sprinkle in the flour and stir for a minute. Pour in the hot stock, whisk until it comes to the boil, then simmer on a medium-high heat, stirring occasionally, until smooth and thickened and the sauce is clear (see tip).

7 Pour in the cream and lemon juice with the cooking juices from the meat and season with salt and pepper. Add the chopped parsley and serve hot with the stuffed chicken thighs.

## MARY'S FOOLPROOF TIP

Vigorous whisking and having piping-hot chicken stock are the key to making this really smooth, velvety sauce.

# THAI CHICKEN CURRY

**A winning combination of textures and flavours, this is good enough to serve for a special occasion. Giving a lovely crunch to the dish, the water chestnuts should be added at the end so they stay crisp.**

Serves 8

PREPARE AHEAD
Make the curry up to a day ahead, adding the freshly cooked peas and water chestnuts just before serving.

FREEZE
This dish freezes well without the sugar snap peas and water chestnuts; add these to the curry after reheating.

6 skinless and boneless chicken breasts

3 tbsp Thai red curry paste

3 tbsp sunflower oil

2 onions, sliced

4cm (1½in) knob of fresh root ginger, peeled and finely grated (see tip on page 187)

1 rounded tbsp plain flour

2 x 400g tins of full-fat coconut milk

1 tbsp Thai fish sauce

1 tbsp light muscovado sugar

1 lemon grass stalk, bashed (see tip)

4 Kaffir lime leaves

250g (9oz) sugar snap peas, cut in half lengthways

finely grated zest and juice of ½ lime

1 x 225g tin of water chestnuts, drained, halved and quartered if large

salt and freshly ground black pepper

1 Cut the chicken breasts in half and then into long thin slices. Tip into a bowl and add 1 tablespoon of the Thai curry paste, season with salt and pepper and mix to combine.

2 Heat 1 tablespoon of the sunflower oil in a deep frying pan, add the chicken slices and fry over a high heat for 5 minutes until just cooked through (avoid overcooking it) – you may need to do this in batches. Using a slotted spoon, transfer the cooked chicken slices to a plate.

3 Add the remaining oil to the pan, tip in the onions and fry for 3 minutes. Cover with a lid, lower the heat and cook for another 10 minutes to soften.

4 Increase the heat, add the ginger with the remaining Thai curry paste and fry for a minute. Sprinkle in the flour and blend in the coconut milk with the fish sauce and sugar, adding a little at a time. Stir the mixture and bring to the boil. Add the lemon grass and lime leaves and season with salt and pepper. Return the chicken to the pan, bring back up to the boil and then cover, reduce the heat and simmer for about 5 minutes until piping hot.

5 Meanwhile, cook the sugar snap peas in boiling salted water for 2 minutes, drain and refresh in cold water.

6 Remove the lemon grass and lime leaves from the curry and discard. Add the lime zest and juice, water chestnuts and sugar snap peas. Bring to the boil, then remove from the heat and serve with rice.

## MARY'S FOOLPROOF TIP

The flavour of lemon grass is wonderful, but the chopped stalk takes a long time to tenderise. I therefore like to bash it with a rolling pin before adding it to the curry – this allows all the flavours to be absorbed into the sauce.

# CHICKEN, RED WINE AND GARLIC CASSEROLE

**My version of coq au vin, this is just the dish for serving on a cold day.**

Serves 6

PREPARE AHEAD
Can be made up to 3 days ahead and kept in the fridge.

FREEZE
Freezes well for up to a month. Thaw and reheat to add the fried mushrooms.

400g (14oz) baby shallots, peeled (see tip)

3 garlic cloves, crushed

1 small bunch of thyme

4 bay leaves

600ml (1 pint) red wine

6 small skinless and boneless chicken breasts

2 tbsp olive oil

75g (3oz) butter

3 tbsp plain flour

350g (12oz) smoked streaky bacon, chopped into pieces

1 tbsp tomato purée

1 tbsp light muscovado sugar

400g (14oz) button mushrooms, halved

salt and freshly ground black pepper

1 Place the shallots in a large bowl with the garlic and herbs. Pour in the wine and mix together. Add the chicken breasts, season and leave to marinate for a minimum of 1 hour. When you're ready to cook, preheat the oven to 160°C/140°C fan/Gas 3.

2 Sit a colander over a large saucepan and strain the marinated chicken, reserving the shallots, bay leaves and thyme. Dab the chicken with kitchen paper to dry it.

3 Heat the oil and 50g (2oz) of the butter in a deep ovenproof frying pan or casserole dish. Add the chicken breasts and fry on each side on a medium-high heat, for 5–10 minutes, until browned all over – you may need to do this in batches. Remove with a slotted spoon and set aside.

4 Meanwhile, set the pan with the wine marinade over a high heat and boil, for 5–10 minutes, so that it reduces to 400ml (14fl oz). Measure the flour into a bowl, add 150ml (5fl oz) of water and whisk until smooth before stirring in a little of the hot wine and then adding this mixture to the rest of the wine in the pan. Keep hot.

5 Add the bacon to the frying pan or casserole dish and fry over a high heat – in batches, if needed – for about 10 minutes until browned, then tip in the reserved shallots and continue to cook for another 10 minutes, until starting to soften.

6 Add the hot wine sauce and tomato purée with the sugar, reserved bay leaves and thyme. Season with salt and pepper and bring to a boil, stir until thickened and add the browned chicken. Bring back to the boil, cover with a lid and transfer to the oven to bake for 20–25 minutes until cooked through.

7 Meanwhile, melt the remaining butter in a pan and fry the mushrooms over a medium heat for 5–10 minutes until just cooked, then add to the chicken casserole just before serving. Remove the bay leaves and thyme from the casserole and serve the casserole hot with mashed potato and shredded cabbage.

## MARY'S FOOLPROOF TIP

To peel shallots more easily, soak them in boiling water for 5 minutes before peeling.

# WHOLE ROAST CHICKEN WITH LEMON AND HERBS

**This delicious roast chicken, infused with wonderful flavours from lemon and herbs, is perfect for a Sunday roast at any time of year. If you have any stalks left over from the herbs, put them in the cavity of the bird.**

Serves 6

PREPARE AHEAD

Can be spread with herb butter and kept in the fridge for up to a day before roasting. To serve cold, roast up to 2 days ahead. The gravy can be stored in the fridge for use the following day with any leftovers.

1 large chicken (1.5–2kg/3lb–4lb 6oz)

3–4 tbsp plain flour

100ml (3½fl oz) white wine

400ml (14fl oz) chicken stock

a few drops of gravy browning (optional)

FOR THE HERB BUTTER

2 garlic cloves, crushed

1 tbsp finely chopped rosemary leaves

1 tbsp finely chopped thyme leaves

2 tbsp finely chopped parsley

50g (2oz) butter, softened

1 lemon, zest finely grated (retaining the lemon)

salt and freshly ground black pepper

1 Preheat the oven to 200°C/180°C fan/Gas 6.

2 First make the herb butter. Tip the garlic and chopped herbs into a bowl, add the butter and lemon zest and season with salt and pepper. Mash together with a fork, mixing well to combine.

3 Pull up the skin over the chicken breast and push half the herb butter under it. Rub the remainder over the top of the chicken and the legs. Cut the zested lemon in half and squeeze one half over the chicken, then insert into the chicken cavity.

4 Place a rack in a roasting tin and sit the prepared chicken on top. Roast in the oven for 1½–2 hours (see tip) until the meat is cooked through but not dry (see tip). Remove from the tin and transfer to a board, cover with foil and leave to rest for 10 minutes.

5 Take the tin containing all the cooking juices from the chicken, and place on the hob over a medium-high heat. Sprinkle over the flour and whisk until smooth, then add the wine and stock and whisk until combined and bubbling. Add a few drops of graving browning, if you like. Pass the gravy through a sieve to remove any lumps, and adjust the seasoning, adding salt and pepper to taste.

6 Carve the chicken and serve with the gravy.

## MARY'S FOOLPROOF TIPS

Roast the chicken for 20 minutes per 450g (1lb)/45 minutes per 1kg (2lb 3oz), plus an additional 20 minutes.

To test if the chicken is cooked, insert a small sharp knife into the thickest part of the thigh; if the juices run clear, it is done.

# FOOLPROOF POULTRY

Chicken is one of my go-to meats for everyday cooking. It's affordable, versatile and relatively low in fat; it can be easily whipped up into a tasty midweek family supper or transformed into a special feast with the addition of just a few simple ingredients.

Chicken and other poultry may be versatile, but they still require careful cooking in order to make the most of the delicate flavours and ensure it is as tender and juicy as it can be. Cooking time is key: too long and the meat will be dry and tough; too short and you risk undercooking the meat, which can lead to food poisoning. Unlike many other meats, poultry must be cooked through. If you stick to these simple rules, you'll have perfect results every time.

## CHOOSING, BUYING AND HANDLING

### DO . . .

*Buy the best-quality chicken you can afford* to ensure the finest flavour. A slowly reared, free-range or organic bird is ideal.

*Keep it cool* Store in the fridge.

*Keep things clean* Ensure work surfaces and any equipment – boards or knives – used in the preparation of the meat are thoroughly washed after use.

*Take care when defrosting* All frozen chicken needs to defrost slowly in the fridge, which can take some time. You'll need to allow about 24 hours for every 2.3kg (5lb) of meat to ensure that it's thoroughly defrosted before cooking. A large turkey can take up to 48 hours to defrost in the fridge, so make sure you allow enough time.

*Remove any packaging* from whole birds or portions. Absorb any moisture with kitchen paper. Transfer to a clean dish, loosely cover in cling film and store in the fridge until needed.

### DON'T . . .

*Forget to wash your hands* Hygiene is crucial when preparing any food and is especially important when handling meat. Wash your hands thoroughly with warm soapy water after handling raw meat.

## COOKING

### DO . . .

*Remove any string* from whole birds before roasting. And check for any giblets that may be left inside the bird; remove these and discard, or use to make stock, if you like.

*Remove any excess fat or sinew* from chicken legs before cooking.

*Ensure the bird's skin is dry before roasting* Pat dry with kitchen paper to mop up any excess moisture. This will help to create crispy skin.

*Cover the breasts of whole birds with streaky bacon rashers or butter* This keeps the breast basted with fat while roasting and helps prevent the meat from drying out.

This method works particularly well with game birds like pheasant and guinea fowl, which tend to be leaner than chicken.

*Cook on the bone* Where possible, cook chicken on the bone as this adds flavour to the meat during cooking.

DON'T . . .

*Carve straight away* Always allow a roasted bird to rest. Resting time can make all the difference to the succulence of the meat. Allow the bird to sit for at least 15 minutes before carving; this makes it juicier.

*Forget to check the meat is cooked through* To test if a roast chicken is cooked, pierce the thickest part of the leg (thigh) with a metal skewer – the juices should run clear. If there is any blood in the juices, return the bird to the oven; check every 5–10 minutes until it is cooked.

CUTS OF CHICKEN

*A whole chicken* can be cooked fast or slowly, either roasted in a hot oven for around an hour or poached gently in a simmering pan of stock for 1½–2 hours.

*Spatchcocking* a chicken (removing the backbone and opening it out like a book) allows the whole bird to be cooked more quickly. This method works especially well when barbecuing chicken or for poussins (young chickens).

*Thighs and drumsticks* contain more fat than the breast meat and therefore stand up well to long, slow cooking in casseroles and stews. They can also be roasted, grilled or barbecued and the meat remains succulent because of the higher fat content.

*Chicken breasts* are very lean and require careful cooking to ensure the meat doesn't dry out or become tough. They are best cooked quickly over a high heat to prevent loss of moisture.

HOW TO MAKE CHICKEN STOCK

If you are roasting a chicken, it's well worth using the leftover carcass to create a wonderful homemade stock. You can also use raw chicken bones to make a stock, but it's important that you don't mix these with cooked bones. The depth of flavour of a homemade stock is incomparable to ready-made versions and it can be frozen for later use – divided into smaller portions, if you like – ready to add to risottos, soups and casseroles. Chicken bones can also be frozen to make stock at a later date when you have more time, if you prefer.

*1* Remove any meat from the roast chicken carcass and set aside to eat as leftovers.

*2* Break the chicken carcass into smaller pieces and transfer to a large casserole dish or saucepan, along with any skin and fat.

*3* Add a chopped onion and carrot, a bay leaf and a few black peppercorns. You can also add a few parsley stalks or thyme sprigs and some roughly chopped leek or celery, if you have any, but they are not crucial. Cover with cold water.

*4* Bring to the boil, then reduce the heat and simmer, uncovered, for at least 2 but preferably 3 hours, skimming off any scum as it rises to the surface. Strain the stock through a fine sieve. Allow to cool, then chill in the fridge or freeze for up to 3 months.

# TURKEY WALDORF SALAD

**A great way of using up leftover turkey at Christmas or cooked chicken from a regular Sunday roast. The salad looks more attractive if you use turkey that's been pulled into pieces rather than neatly cut.**

Serves 6

PREPARE AHEAD
The dressing can be made up to a day ahead.

500g (1lb 2oz) cooked turkey

1 eating apple (unpeeled)

2 romaine lettuces

juice of ½ lemon

2 celery sticks, thinly sliced

50g (2oz) walnut pieces, toasted (see tip on page 237)

seeds from 1 small pomegranate (see tip)

chunky bread, to serve

FOR THE DRESSING

150g (5oz) Stilton cheese, roughly chopped

150g (5oz) soured cream

juice of ½ lemon

salt and freshly ground black pepper

1 Using your hands, pull the turkey into long thin strips and then tip into a bowl. To make the dressing, measure the Stilton and soured cream into a food processor, add the lemon juice, season with salt and pepper and whizz to combine. Pour half this dressing into the bowl with the turkey strips. Toss together and leave to marinate for about an hour.

2 Core the apple and cut into thin slices, then pour over the remaining lemon juice to prevent the apple from going brown.

3 To assemble the salad, shred the lettuces and spread the leaves over the base of a large, open platter. Scatter over the celery and apple slices, followed by the toasted walnut pieces, and season with salt and pepper. Spoon over the remaining dressing, then add the marinated turkey and scatter with pomegranate seeds.

4 Toss together and serve with chunky bread.

## MARY'S FOOLPROOF TIP

To extract the seeds easily from a pomegranate, cut the fruit in half and use a wooden spoon to firmly tap the hard shell. The seeds should fall out.

# HOT TURKEY AND AVOCADO BAKE

This bake is quick, easy and very, very delicious! It may seem an unusual combination but is really just a twist on the classic chicken and avocado – ideal for using up leftover roast turkey, and a bit different from a pie. Serve with a dressed green salad and crunchy bread.

Serves 6

PREPARE AHEAD
Can be assembled up to 12 hours ahead, then sprinkled with the crisps and baked to serve.

2 celery sticks, sliced

4 spring onions, sliced

300ml (10fl oz) full-fat mayonnaise

juice of 1 lemon

100g (4oz) mature Cheddar cheese, grated

flesh of 1 large avocado, cut into cubes

350g (12oz) cooked turkey, cut into small cubes (see tip)

300g (11oz) cherry tomatoes, halved

2 tbsp chopped parsley

1 x 30g packet of ready salted crisps, crushed into tiny crumbs

paprika, for sprinkling

salt and freshly ground black pepper

1 Preheat the oven to 200°C/180°C fan/Gas 6. You will need a 1.1-litre (2-pint) wide-based, shallow ovenproof dish.

2 Tip the celery and spring onions into a large bowl, then add the mayonnaise, half the lemon juice and two-thirds of the grated cheese, season with salt and pepper and toss together.

3 Toss the avocado cubes in the remaining lemon juice (see tip on page 25) and add to the bowl with the turkey, tomatoes and parsley. Carefully mix together and then spoon into the ovenproof dish. Scatter with the remaining cheese and the crushed crisps and sprinkle with paprika.

4 Bake in the oven for 12–15 minutes until golden and piping hot in the middle (see tip). Do not allow it to boil, otherwise it will separate. As it takes such a short time to cook, it is best served straight from the oven.

## MARY'S FOOLPROOF TIPS

Choose an avocado that is firm and just ripe, otherwise the cubes will not keep their shape.

I always assemble this turkey dish ahead and then bake it to serve straight away. Sometimes I use leftover chicken in place of the turkey – it is a winner!

# VENISON STEAKS WITH BLACKBERRY SAUCE AND ROASTED VEGETABLES

**A hearty, country dish with a modern twist, this would be lovely for serving on a wintry day.**

Serves 6

PREPARE AHEAD
The sauce can be made up to a day ahead.

1 small celeriac (600g/1lb 5oz), peeled and cut into 1.5cm (⅝in) cubes

1 small butternut squash (1kg/2lb 3oz), peeled, deseeded and cut into 1.5cm (⅝in) cubes

3 tbsp olive oil

1 tbsp chopped thyme leaves

6 x 125g (4½oz) venison steaks

salt and freshly ground black pepper

thyme sprigs, to garnish

FOR THE SAUCE

a knob of butter

1 onion, roughly chopped

3 tbsp plain flour

150ml (5fl oz) port or Madeira

350ml (12fl oz) chicken stock

2 tbsp blackberry jam or jelly

a dash of gravy browning

100g (4oz) blackberries

1 Preheat the oven to 220°C/200°C fan/Gas 7.

2 Put the celeriac and squash into a roasting tin in a single layer, and drizzle over half the oil. Season with salt and pepper and toss to coat in the oil. Roast in the oven for about 30 minutes, until tender and crisp, then sprinkle with thyme.

3 After the vegetables have been roasting for about 5 minutes, prepare the rest of the dish (see tip). To make the sauce, melt the butter in a wide-based saucepan, add the onion and fry over a high heat for 2–3 minutes. Reduce the heat to low, cover with a lid and continue to cook for about 10 minutes until softened. Remove the lid and cook for a few minutes to allow any liquid to evaporate.

4 Sprinkle over the flour and stir in, then gradually add the port or Madeira and stock, gently whisking all the time, until you have a smooth sauce. Bring to the boil, stirring, until the sauce is thickened. Add the jam or jelly and the dash of gravy browning, and remove from the heat.

5 Place a large frying pan over a high heat. Coat the venison steaks in the remaining oil and season with salt and pepper. Fry over a high heat for about 3 minutes on each side until brown on the outside but pink in the middle. Transfer to a warm plate, cover with foil and leave to rest.

6 Return the sauce to the heat. Tip in any meat juices from the plate of venison, check the seasoning, adding salt and pepper to taste, and bring back up to the boil. Strain the sauce to remove any lumps, then stir through the blackberries.

7 Divide the roasted root vegetables between individual plates, then carve the venison steaks into thin slices and arrange on each plate. Spoon over the hot sauce and garnish with thyme sprigs to serve.

## MARY'S FOOLPROOF TIP

It is important to time each element of the dish so that everything is hot at the same time. It is a great help to make the sauce ahead and reheat.

# TWO-HOUR GAME BOLOGNAISE

Unlike a beef bolognaise, this has a deep gamey flavour and needs long, slow cooking. You can buy convenient game casserole packs in supermarkets. If buying from your local butcher, ask for a mixture of your favourite game – pheasant, guinea fowl, rabbit, venison, partridge. If you're short of time, you can always ask your butcher to dice the meat for you.

Serves 6

**PREPARE AHEAD**
The bolognaise can be made up to 2 days ahead and reheated to serve.

**FREEZE**
Freezes well cooked.

3 tbsp oil

750g (1lb 10oz) mixed game meat, diced into 2cm (¾in) cubes

1 large onion, chopped

2 small carrots, peeled and finely chopped

150g (5oz) chestnut mushrooms, finely diced

2 garlic cloves, crushed

1 tbsp light muscovado sugar

2 tbsp tomato purée

300ml (10fl oz) red wine

1 x 400g tin of chopped tomatoes

200ml (7fl oz) beef stock

1 tbsp finely chopped rosemary leaves

3 bay leaves

500g (1lb 2oz) spaghetti

salt and freshly ground black pepper

Parmesan cheese, freshly grated, to serve (optional)

1 Preheat the oven to 150°C/130°C fan/Gas 2.

2 Heat the oil in a large, ovenproof frying pan or casserole dish, add the diced meat and cook – in batches, if necessary – over a high heat until golden and sealed. Transfer to a plate and set aside.

3 Add the onion and carrots to the frying pan, plus a little extra oil if needed, and fry over a high heat for about 5 minutes until starting to brown. Add the mushroom and garlic and fry for a further 5 minutes, until the mushrooms have softened.

4 Return the game to the pan, sprinkle in the sugar, add the tomato purée and fry for a minute. Pour in the wine, tomatoes and stock, add the herbs and season with salt and pepper. Bring to the boil, then cover with a lid and transfer to the oven to cook for about 2 hours or until the meat is falling apart (see tip). Add a little more stock at this point if the bolognaise is looking a little dry.

5 Shortly before the bolognaise has finished cooking, bring a pan of salted water to the boil and cook the spaghetti according to the packet instructions. Drain well, transfer to plates and serve with the bolognaise spooned on top and a sprinkling of grated Parmesan, if you like.

## MARY'S FOOLPROOF TIP

This is all about long, slow cooking of the game. Because different meats are being used, they need to cook for a long time until each of them is falling apart and tender.

# PORK, BEEF & LAMB

# PORK, APPLE AND STILTON PARCELS

Perfect for a weekday supper, Black Forest ham would work well in this recipe as an alternative to Parma ham, if you preferred.

Serves 4

PREPARE AHEAD
Can be assembled up to 6 hours ahead, ready to roast.

4 boneless pork loin chops

1 tbsp oil, plus extra oil for greasing

1 tbsp runny honey

8 slices of Parma ham

1 small eating apple, peeled, cored and thinly sliced

100g (4oz) Stilton cheese, sliced

4 large sage leaves, chopped

salt and freshly ground black pepper

**1** Preheat the oven to 200°C/180°C fan/Gas 6 and grease a baking tray with a little extra oil.

**2** Season each pork chop with salt and pepper, and cut off any surplus fat. Heat the oil in a large frying pan over a high heat, add the chops, pour over the honey (see tip) and brown for 1–2 minutes on each side. You may need to do this in two batches, using half the honey each time. Remove and set aside to cool.

**3** Lay two slices of the Parma ham together on a chopping board, overlapping them along one edge. Place one browned chop in the middle of the ham, add a quarter of the apple and Stilton slices and a sprinkling of chopped sage.

**4** Fold the ham around the chop to create a parcel and repeat with the remaining ingredients to create four parcels.

**5** Place on the prepared baking tray and cook in the oven for 15–20 minutes or until the pork is cooked and the Parma ham is crispy. Serve hot with the juices in the pan.

## MARY'S FOOLPROOF TIP

The honey helps the pork to brown quickly; if it's not included, there is a tendency to keep cooking the pork until it is brown, leading to overcooking.

# PORK CHOPS WITH MUSHROOM CRUST

These are lovely for a midweek supper and ideal for preparing ahead.
Serve hot with green vegetables and buttered new potatoes.

Serves 6

**PREPARE AHEAD**
Can be assembled up to 8 hours ahead, ready for the oven. Cover with foil and keep in the fridge until ready to cook.

2 tbsp olive oil

6 x 225g (8oz) pork loin chops on the bone, rind removed

a knob of butter

2 onions, thinly sliced

250g (9oz) chestnut mushrooms, thinly sliced

1 tbsp Dijon mustard

50g (2oz) panko breadcrumbs

100g (4oz) mature Cheddar cheese, grated

a pinch of paprika

salt and freshly ground black pepper

**1** Preheat the oven to 200°C/180°C fan/Gas 6.

**2** Add the oil to a large frying pan set over a high heat. Season the chops with salt and pepper and brown on each side for a few minutes until golden (see tip) – you may need to do this in batches. Transfer to a baking tray or shallow roasting tin, and leave to cool down completely.

**3** Melt the butter in the frying pan, add the onions and fry over a high heat for 3 minutes. Cover the pan with a lid, reduce the heat to low and cook for 10–15 minutes or until softened and golden. Remove the lid, increasing the heat to drive off any moisture, then add the mushrooms and fry over a high heat for 5 minutes or until all the liquid has evaporated. Season with salt and pepper.

**4** Spread the mustard on the cold pork chops and spoon the mushroom mixture on top – dividing it evenly between the chops. Sprinkle with the breadcrumbs, grated cheese and paprika.

**5** Bake in the oven for about 15 minutes or until a golden crust has formed and the chops are cooked through. Serve with new potatoes and buttered cabbage.

## MARY'S FOOLPROOF TIP

Brown the pork on all sides, including the fatty edges. This seals the juices in and prevents the pork from drying out during baking.

# SAUSAGE AND ONION CASSOULET

Sausages cooked with butter beans in a flavoursome, hearty dish that should go down very well with the whole family!

| Serves 4–6 | PREPARE AHEAD | FREEZE |
| --- | --- | --- |
| | Can be made up to a day ahead and reheated to serve. | Suitable for freezing for up to a month without the beans. |

1 tbsp oil

12 pork sausages

3 large onions, thinly sliced

1 garlic clove, finely chopped

1 tbsp plain flour

250ml (9fl oz) white wine

250ml (9fl oz) chicken stock

2 bay leaves

6 sprigs of thyme

2 x 400g tins of butter beans, drained and rinsed

salt and freshly ground black pepper

**1** Preheat the oven 180°C/160°C fan/Gas 4.

**2** Heat the oil in a large, very deep frying pan or shallow casserole dish and fry the sausages on a medium heat, turning all the time, until dark golden brown (see tip). Remove with a slotted spoon and set aside.

**3** Add the onions to the same pan (no need to wash) and fry over a high heat for about 3 minutes until beginning to soften. Add the garlic and fry for another minute.

**4** Sprinkle in the flour, stirring it into the onions, then pour in the wine and bring to the boil, stirring all the while. Add the stock and bring back up to the boil, stirring continuously. Add the bay leaves, thyme sprigs and fried sausages. Season with salt and pepper, add the drained beans and bring back up to the boil again.

**5** Cover the pan or dish with a lid and transfer to the oven to bake for about 30 minutes until the sausages are cooked. Remove the bay leaves and thyme sprigs and serve piping hot.

## MARY'S FOOLPROOF TIP

It's so important to really brown the sausages first. This creates a wonderful flavour as well as colour – if the sausages are pale, the dish won't look nearly so attractive.

# PORK FILLET PIE WITH MUSHROOMS AND MASH

*A bit like a cottage or shepherd's pie but using pork fillet instead of minced beef or lamb.*
*This needs short cooking; other cuts of meat would need long, slow cooking.*

Serves 6–8

PREPARE AHEAD
Can be assembled up to 8 hours ahead and cooked to serve.

3 tbsp oil

750g (1lb 10oz) pork fillet, cut into 1cm (½in) cubes

1 onion, finely sliced

2 garlic cloves, crushed

300g (11oz) chestnut mushrooms, quartered

30g (1oz) plain flour

150ml (5fl oz) apple juice

150ml (5fl oz) beef stock

200ml (7fl oz) crème fraîche

2 tsp finely chopped rosemary leaves

salt and freshly ground black pepper

## FOR THE TOPPING

1kg (2lb 3oz) floury potatoes, peeled and chopped

30g (1oz) butter

4 tbsp milk

50g (2oz) Cheddar cheese, grated

1 You will need a 2–2.25-litre (3½–4-pint) wide-based ovenproof dish.

2 Heat 2 tablespoons of the oil in a large, deep frying pan and brown the pork in batches over a high heat for just 2–3 minutes until golden and sealed. Using a slotted spoon, transfer the cooked meat to a plate.

3 Heat the remaining oil in the pan, then add the onion and fry over a medium-high heat for 3 minutes. Add the garlic, then cover with a lid, lower the heat and cook for about 15 minutes until tender.

4 Add the mushrooms to the onions and fry, uncovered, over a high heat for 5 minutes. Sprinkle in the flour and stir in, then pour in the apple juice and stock. Bring to the boil and then add the crème fraîche, stirring all the while. Add the rosemary, then season with salt and pepper and return the pork to the pan. Bring back up to the boil and leave to bubble for about 3 minutes. Tip into the ovenproof dish and set aside to cool down completely (see tip).

5 Preheat the oven to 200°C/180°C fan/Gas 6.

6 For the topping, cook the potatoes in boiling salted water for 15–20 minutes until tender. Drain (see tip), then mash the potatoes until smooth with the butter and milk, seasoning to taste with salt and pepper.

7 Spread the mashed potato over the cold pork mixture and sprinkle with the grated cheese. Bake in the oven for 30–35 minutes or until piping hot, then serve with a green vegetable.

## MARY'S FOOLPROOF TIPS

The pork mixture needs to be cold because it's easier to spread hot mashed potato over a cold filling.

Return the potatoes to the heat after straining to help dry them out, then add the butter and milk and heat through to make the mash drier and give it the best consistency. This will help to prevent the sauce leaking through.

# ROAST RACK OF PORK WITH SAGE AND LEMON RUB

Cut from the fore end of the loin, this large joint of pork would be lovely for Sunday lunch. Serve with roast potatoes or puréed swede and a green vegetable. If there is any meat left over, you could serve it cold the next day.

Serves 6

PREPARE AHEAD
The pork can be cooked up to 2 days ahead if serving cold.

2 onions, thickly sliced (about 1cm/½in thick)

1.7kg (3¾lb) forerib of pork loin, skin scored

4 tbsp finely chopped sage leaves

finely grated zest of 1 lemon

coarse sea salt

## FOR THE GRAVY

25g (1oz) butter

25g (1oz) plain flour

1 tsp lemon juice

1 tsp redcurrant jelly

a dash of Worcestershire sauce

salt and freshly ground black pepper

**1** Preheat the oven to 220°C/200°C fan/Gas 7.

**2** Put the onion slices into a small roasting tin, sit the pork joint on top of the onions and rub 1½–2 tablespoons of coarse salt into the scored skin.

**3** Place the sage in a bowl with the lemon zest and ½ tablespoon of coarse salt. Mix together and, using your fingers, rub the mixture into the skin of the joint.

**4** Roast in the oven for 30 minutes until golden and starting to crisp. Reduce the oven temperature to 200°C/180°C fan/Gas 6 and continue to roast for 1 hour and 25 minutes to 1 hour and 35 minutes or until the pork is cooked through, the juices are running clear, and the crackling is crisp and golden (see tip). Carefully remove the pork joint from the tin and set aside to rest for about 10 minutes, covered with foil.

**5** While the meat is resting, make the gravy. Add 450ml (15fl oz) of water to the roasting tin and bring to the boil on the hob, scraping the base of the tin with a wooden spoon to incorporate the caramelised juices into the liquid to create a stock. Remove from the heat and strain into a jug.

**6** Melt the butter in a saucepan, add the flour and whisk to form a roux. Cook for 30 seconds, then blend in the homemade stock over a high heat, whisking all the time and boiling until thickened. Season to taste with salt and pepper, the lemon juice, redcurrant jelly and a dash of Worcestershire sauce.

**7** Carve the pork and crackling and serve with the gravy.

## MARY'S FOOLPROOF TIP

A hot oven and salt give the best crackling. If yours is not quite crisp enough, slice off the crackling with a knife, lay it on a baking sheet and return to the hot oven to crisp up.

# ROAST GAMMON WITH MUSTARD AND ORANGE SAUCE

This delicious joint of succulent roast gammon is perfectly complemented by the tangy sauce. Equally good hot or cold, it is great for serving a crowd.

Serves 10

**PREPARE AHEAD**
Gammon can be roasted up to 4 days ahead if serving cold. Wrapped well in foil, the meat will keep hot for an hour after removing from the oven.

1 x 2kg (4lb 6oz) smoked gammon joint
250ml (9fl oz) orange juice
3 tbsp runny honey
4 tbsp grainy mustard
2 tsp cornflour
200ml (7fl oz) full-fat crème fraîche
salt and freshly ground black pepper

**1** Preheat the oven to 200°C/180°C fan/Gas 6.

**2** Sit the gammon joint in a small roasting tin. Pour 150ml (5fl oz) of the orange juice into the tin and cover the joint loosely with foil.

**3** Roast in the oven for about 2½ hours (see tip).

**4** Remove from the oven and carefully peel or cut away the skin and discard, leaving a thin layer of fat over the meat. Score the fat in diagonal lines across the joint. Take a strip of foil and cover the sides of the meat to stop them drying out when returned to the oven.

**5** Mix together 1 tablespoon of the honey and half the mustard in a small bowl and spread over the scored fat. Return the meat to the oven to roast for another 15 minutes or until the top is brown and glazed. Remove the gammon from the roasting tin and leave to rest for 10 minutes, covered with foil.

**6** Measure the cornflour into a bowl, add 3 tablespoons of cold water and mix until smooth (see tip). Pour the remaining orange juice into the roasting tin and place on the hob. Whisk the orange juice with the cooking juices in the tin, then add the crème fraîche with the remaining honey and mustard. Mix until smooth, then add the cornflour mixture and bring to the boil, whisking until smooth and thickened slightly. Taste and season with salt and pepper if needed. Pour into a jug ready to serve.

**7** Carve the hot gammon into slices and serve with the hot sauce.

## MARY'S FOOLPROOF TIPS

Roast gammon for 30 minutes per 500g (1lb 2oz), plus an extra 30 minutes.

Cornflour is used to thicken the sauce. Be sure to mix it with cold water as hot water would give a lumpy sauce.

# BOILED BEEF AND CARROTS WITH MUSTARD-PARSLEY SAUCE

This old-fashioned dish reminds me of my childhood – my husband, Paul, just loves it! If you have some left over, the beef is delicious cold. You can use salted silverside or salted brisket for this recipe.

Serves 6–8

PREPARE AHEAD
The beef can be cooked up to 2 days ahead if serving cold. The mustard and parsley sauce can be made up to 8 hours ahead and reheated to serve.

1.8kg (4lb) salted silverside of beef (see tip)

450g (1lb) shallots, peeled

600g (1lb 5oz) baby carrots, peeled

2 tbsp chopped parsley, plus extra to garnish

FOR THE SAUCE

50g (2oz) butter

50g (2oz) plain flour

300ml (10fl oz) milk

2 tbsp white wine vinegar

2 tbsp caster sugar

2 tbsp grainy mustard

1 tbsp chopped parsley

salt and freshly ground black pepper

1 Preheat the oven to 160°C/140°C fan/Gas 3.

2 Sit the beef joint in a large, deep ovenproof pan and cover with cold water. Bring to the boil on the hob, then cover with a lid and transfer to the oven to cook for about 2 hours.

3 Remove the pan from the oven and turn the beef in the liquid. Add the vegetables and parsley and bring back up to the boil on the hob. Cover again with the lid and return to the oven for a further 45 minutes–1 hour or until the vegetables are tender.

4 Remove the beef and vegetables from the cooking liquid and keep warm. Measure 300ml (10fl oz) of the hot cooking liquid into a jug (see tip).

5 Next make the sauce. Melt the butter in a saucepan, add the flour and whisk together by hand until blended. Pour in the hot stock slowly, whisking continuously until smooth, and then whisk in the milk. Add the vinegar, sugar and mustard, season with salt and pepper and bring to the boil, whisking until thickened, before adding the parsley.

6 Carve the beef into thin slices and serve with the vegetables, sprinkled with extra parsley, and the mustard-parsley sauce.

## MARY'S FOOLPROOF TIPS

Ask your butcher for salted silverside or brisket. He will brine it for you – usually over the course of a week. Supermarkets have ready-salted joints too, especially in the winter or at Christmas time. Silverside is leaner than brisket.

Keep the remaining cooking liquid, boil it down to reduce it to a flavoursome stock and freeze to use later.

# BEEF WELLINGTON WITH TARRAGON SAUCE

Beef Wellington traditionally has pâté spread over the top of the fillet, in addition to the mushroom stuffing, which makes it very rich. The mushroom mixture here is lighter but with a lovely taste from the tarragon – always buy the French tarragon as Russian tarragon grows well, but has no flavour.

| Serves 6–8 | PREPARE AHEAD | FREEZE |
|---|---|---|
| | The beef Wellington can be prepared up to a day ahead. | Freezes well uncooked. |

1.3kg (2lb 14oz) middle-cut beef fillet (see tip overleaf)

1 tbsp oil

1½ x 375g packets of all-butter puff pastry

plain flour, for dusting

1 egg, beaten with a dash of milk

salt and freshly ground black pepper

FOR THE TOPPING

a large knob of butter

350g (12oz) mixed mushrooms (such as button, chestnut, wild), thinly sliced

50g (2oz) Parmesan cheese, finely grated

1 tbsp finely chopped tarragon

2 tsp Dijon mustard

1 egg yolk

*Ingredients continued*

**1** Preheat the oven to 220°C/200°C fan/Gas 7.

**2** Season the beef with salt and pepper. Place a large frying pan over a high heat, add the oil and fry the beef on all sides until browned. Transfer to a baking tray and roast in the oven for 15–18 minutes. Turn the oven off and remove the beef. Leave to cool, reserving any cooking juices, and then chill in the fridge for at least 1 hour (see tip overleaf).

**3** Next make the mushroom topping. Melt the butter in the same pan and fry the mushrooms over a high heat for 5–10 minutes – you may need to do this in batches. Tip the mushrooms into a sieve set over a bowl to collect the juices and reserve these for the sauce. Transfer the mushrooms to another bowl and allow to cool before mixing with the Parmesan, tarragon, mustard and egg yolk. Season with salt and pepper and chill in the fridge for 30 minutes.

**4** Line a baking sheet with baking paper. Sit the single 375g block of pastry on a floured work surface and roll out to a square about 40cm (16in) in size, then transfer it to the baking sheet. Place the cooked beef to one side of the pastry and spoon the mushroom mixture on top. Fold over the ends of the pastry and then fold the longest edge over the beef, sealing along the side with a little of the egg wash. Chill in the fridge for 30 minutes. While it is chilling, preheat the oven again to 220°C/200°C fan/Gas 7.

**5** Brush the top of the chilled beef Wellington with egg wash. Roll out the remaining half block of pastry and cut into eight thin strips: lay four strips diagonally, and evenly spaced, across the top of the beef Wellington, and four strips across these to create a lattice pattern. Brush the lattice with egg wash and then roast in the oven for 30–35 minutes or until the pastry is golden brown and crisp.

*Continues overleaf*

## FOR THE TARRAGON SAUCE

a small knob of butter

100g (4oz) button mushrooms, finely sliced

1 tbsp plain flour

400ml (14fl oz) full-fat crème fraîche

1 tbsp Dijon mustard

1 tbsp chopped tarragon

a pinch of sugar

# BEEF WELLINGTON WITH TARRAGON SAUCE

*Continued*

**6** Meanwhile, make the tarragon sauce. Melt the butter in the same frying pan and fry the mushrooms over a high heat for 5–10 minutes or until the juices evaporate. Sprinkle in the flour and add the crème fraîche with the reserved mushroom juices (from the topping), the mustard and tarragon. Season with salt, pepper and sugar and bring to the boil, stirring. Simmer for 3 minutes until reduced slightly and add any beef juices from the original baking tray. Keep hot.

**7** Allow the beef Wellington to rest, covered with foil, for 15 minutes before carving. Slice into thick slices and serve with the hot tarragon sauce.

## MARY'S FOOLPROOF TIPS

To ensure even cooking of the beef, try to buy a piece of beef fillet that's from the middle section, with a similar circumference all the way along the piece of meat.

There are lots of chilling stages – this is so important as it ensures the temperature is always correct to give pink, rare beef and cooked pastry. For medium, add 5 minutes to the initial roasting time and for well done, add another 5 minutes.

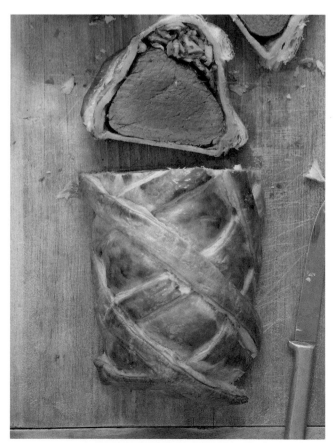

# BEEF STIR-FRY WITH RIBBON VEGETABLES

Quick, healthy and tasty, this is ideal for a midweek supper. I prefer the medium egg noodles, but go with whichever variety you prefer – just follow the cooking instructions on the packet.

Serves 4–6

**PREPARE AHEAD**
The meat can be marinated for up to 8 hours in advance and the vegetables prepared and kept chilled in the fridge for up to 4 hours.

350g (12oz) rump or sirloin steak, cut into thin strips

1 tsp Chinese five-spice powder

6cm (2½in) knob of fresh root ginger, peeled and finely grated (see tip on page 187)

4 garlic cloves, finely chopped

2 small courgettes

2 carrots, peeled

125g (4½oz) dried medium egg noodles

2 tbsp oil

175g (6oz) baby sweetcorn, halved lengthways

4 spring onions, sliced

100g (4oz) mangetout, halved lengthways

50g (2oz) bean sprouts

3 tbsp soy sauce

2 tbsp Thai fish sauce

juice of 1 lime

salt and freshly ground black pepper

**1** Tip the beef strips into a bowl, add the Chinese five spice, ginger and garlic, season with salt and pepper and toss together to coat. Set aside to marinate for 30 minutes.

**2** Meanwhile, prepare the courgettes and carrots, using a vegetable or julienne peeler to cut the vegetables into thin ribbons, peeling from top to bottom (see tip).

**3** Bring a pan of salted water to the boil and cook the egg noodles according to the packet instructions, then drain and set aside.

**4** Heat half the oil in a large, deep frying pan or wok, add the marinated beef and stir-fry over a high heat for 2–4 minutes, stirring, until seared all over but still pink in the middle. Remove with a slotted spoon and set aside.

**5** Add the remaining oil to the pan, followed by the sweetcorn, spring onions and mangetout, and fry for 1 minute. Tip in the courgette and carrot ribbons and stir-fry for a further minute. Add the bean sprouts and drained noodles with the soy and fish sauces and return the seared beef to the pan. Toss over a high heat, season with salt and pepper and pour over the lime juice. Serve immediately while piping hot.

## MARY'S FOOLPROOF TIP

Very quick cooking is important or the beef will overcook and the vegetables will steam. So having all the ingredients prepared in advance is key for quick stir-fry cooking.

# MEXICAN TORTILLA BAKE

This all-in-one dish is so quick to make. Think of a Mexican-inspired lasagne using ready-made tortillas instead of sheets of pasta. This was an idea from my friend and assistant, Lucy Young, and is now a regular bake for all of us. Utterly delicious and very moreish!

**Serves 6**

**PREPARE AHEAD**
The mince can be cooked and the dish assembled up to 6 hours ahead, then baked to serve.

**FREEZE**
Freezes well uncooked.

## FOR THE MINCE
1 tbsp olive oil

2 large onions, chopped

500g (1lb 2oz) lean minced beef

1 fresh mild red chilli, deseeded and finely chopped

1 red pepper, deseeded and diced

2 garlic cloves, crushed

1 tbsp ground cumin

1 tbsp ground coriander

2 tbsp tomato purée

1–2 tbsp mango chutney

2 x 400g tins of chopped tomatoes

1 small bunch of coriander, chopped

salt and freshly ground black pepper

## TO ASSEMBLE
3 large tortilla wraps

250g (9oz) full-fat mascarpone cheese

100g (4oz) mozzarella cheese, grated

100g (4oz) Cheddar cheese, grated

**1** You will need a 1.5-litre (2½-pint) wide-based, shallow ovenproof dish. Preheat the oven to 160°C/140°C fan/Gas 3.

**2** Pour the oil into a large ovenproof frying pan over a medium heat, add the onions and fry for 3 minutes. Turn up the heat, tip in the minced beef and fry over a high heat, breaking the meat up with a wooden spoon and stirring occasionally, until brown.

**3** Add the chilli, red pepper, garlic and spices and fry for about 5 minutes until all the moisture has evaporated and the mixture is quite dry. Stir in the tomato purée, mango chutney and tinned tomatoes and season well with salt and pepper. Cover with a lid, bring to the boil and transfer to the oven to simmer for about an hour.

**4** Remove from the oven and stir in half the coriander. Increase the oven temperature to 200°C/180°C fan/Gas 6.

**5** Spread a third of the cooked minced beef mixture over the bottom of the ovenproof dish and lay one tortilla wrap on top. Spread a third of the mascarpone (see tip) over the tortilla and sprinkle with a third of each of the mozzarella and Cheddar cheeses. Repeat twice more so you have three layers.

**6** Bake in the oven for about 25 minutes until golden and bubbling. Set aside for 5 minutes before serving scattered with the remaining coriander.

## MARY'S FOOLPROOF TIP

If your mascarpone is firm, you might find it easier to spread the mascarpone on each tortilla first before adding to the dish.

# CATALAN BEEF

This hearty, Spanish-themed casserole is full of flavour – just serve with a green vegetable.

| Serves 6 | PREPARE AHEAD | FREEZE |
| --- | --- | --- |
| | Can be made up to 2 days ahead and reheated to serve. | Freezes well, though expect the vegetables to be soft. |

1 tbsp olive oil

150g (5oz) smoked streaky bacon, sliced

1kg (2lb 3oz) diced braising beef

1 large onion, sliced

3 garlic cloves, crushed

80g (3oz) small skinned chorizo sausages, sliced

50g (2oz) plain flour

225ml (8fl oz) white wine

500ml (18fl oz) beef stock

1 x 400g tin of chopped tomatoes

2 tbsp tomato purée

500g (1lb 2oz) baby carrots

350g (12oz) peeled potatoes, chopped into large dice

salt and freshly ground black pepper

**1** Preheat the oven to 160°C/140°C fan/Gas 3.

**2** Heat a large, deep ovenproof pan or casserole dish on the hob, add the oil and bacon and fry over a high heat until crisp. Using a slotted spoon, transfer the cooked bacon to a plate.

**3** Add the beef, in two batches (see tip), to the pan and brown in the bacon fat until lightly browned all over, then remove with the slotted spoon and add to the bacon on the plate. Tip the onion and garlic into the pan and fry for 3–4 minutes. Add the chorizo and fry for 2–3 minutes until crisp.

**4** Measure the flour into a bowl, pour in half the wine and whisk until smooth.

**5** Add the stock to the pan with the tinned tomatoes and remaining wine. Tip in the flour mixture, bring to the boil and stir until smooth and thickened. Add the tomato purée and season with salt and pepper. Return the cooked bacon and beef to the pan, cover with a lid and bring back up to the boil.

**6** Transfer to the oven to cook for 1 hour, then remove from the oven, add the carrots and potatoes and bring back up to the boil on the hob. Cover again with the lid and return to the oven to cook for another 1–1¼ hours or until the beef, potatoes and carrots are tender. Season to taste with salt and pepper and add a little hot water if the sauce is too thick.

## MARY'S FOOLPROOF TIP

Browning the beef in two batches is better than trying to crowd the whole amount into the pan at once. It keeps the pan at a good hot temperature, and allows the meat to get well browned, to add flavour to the dish.

# FOOLPROOF MEAT

Whether enjoyed as traditional British classics or as new, exciting dishes from around the world, pork, beef and lamb remain firm favourites in my family. From satisfying weekday suppers and comforting casseroles to impressive dinner party dishes and Sunday roasts, the possibilities with these meats are endless.

COOKING MEAT As with all meat, the cooking method and the timing are the two most important things to get right. So long as you choose the correct method of cooking for the cut of meat you are using, you can't go too wrong. The following basic cooking techniques can be applied to pork, beef or lamb.

ROASTING Roasting is the method best suited to cooking large joints of meat. For a classic fast roast (such as a loin of pork, rib of beef or leg of lamb) the oven temperature starts off very high (around 220°C/200°C fan/Gas 7) for the initial 15–30 minutes (depending on the size of the joint) to kick-start the cooking process, then the temperature is reduced to around 180°C/160°C fan/Gas 4 for the remainder of the cooking time. Slow roasting is often used for fattier, cheaper joints of meat – for example, shoulder of lamb, belly of pork or silverside of beef. Here the joint is cooked for a few hours at a very low temperature to allow it to tenderise and to keep the fat permeated throughout the meat. This results in melt-in-the-mouth meat, so tender that it falls away from the bone and is effortless to carve.

DO . . .

*Preheat the oven* for at least 15 minutes before roasting.

*Choose the right tin* If the tin is too large, the juices will spread too thinly and burn, which would lose any potential base for making gravy, so it's important to pick an appropriate-sized roasting tin for the joint.

*Cook meat on the bone where possible* The bone conducts heat and cooks the meat from the inside out, which helps retain juiciness and flavour.

*Use the meat juices to make gravy* There is so much flavour in the roasting juices and they make the perfect base for a tasty gravy. First skim off any excess fat, then, over the heat on the hob, add a splash of wine to deglaze the roasting tin and dislodge any meat residue from the base of the tin. Add boiling water, or vegetable cooking water, and simmer to make a delicious gravy.

DON'T . . .

*Use a blunt knife for carving* A sharp knife will make carving even, thin slices much easier.

***Skimp on resting time*** Larger joints may need to rest for up to 30 minutes to allow the meat to relax and become tender.

## FOOLPROOF PORK CRACKLING

Follow these four steps to make perfect pork crackling:

***1 Ensure the pork skin is evenly scored*** You can ask your butcher to do this for you or use a very sharp kitchen or retractable-blade knife.

***2 Dry the skin with kitchen paper, rub with oil and season with salt*** Massage the skin with a little cooking oil before rubbing plenty of coarse salt into the scored skin.

***3 Ensure the oven is fully preheated to a high temperature*** before roasting the pork. The meat usually needs at least 30 minutes at a very high temperature (around 220°C/200°C fan/Gas 7) to make the skin crackle successfully.

***4 Roast it separately*** If you are struggling to achieve good crackling, you can remove the skin from the cooked pork. Slip a sharp knife under the skin, lay it on a baking tray, return to a hot oven and cook until crisp while the meat is resting.

## BRAISING OR CASSEROLING

Slowly braising tougher and fattier cuts transforms them into tender, succulent meat. Casseroles, stews and one pots work by gently simmering chunks of meat in a flavoursome liquid over a few hours until the muscle fibres have broken down and the meat has become soft and flavoursome. Neck and shoulder of lamb, beef shin, skirt or chuck steak, oxtail and shoulder of pork are all cuts that lend themselves to slow cooking.

### DO . . .

***Sear the meat in small batches*** It's important to initially sear the meat all over to help seal in the moisture; it is also more visually appealing when the meat is browned. Cook the meat, a few pieces at a time, in a preheated saucepan or casserole dish over a high heat; don't overcrowd the pan as this will reduce the overall temperature and the meat will steam rather than sear.

***Simmer gently*** Once the stock has been added, bring to the boil and then reduce the temperature to very low. The meat needs to cook very gently and slowly or it will toughen rather than tenderise.

## FRYING

Frying is one of the quickest and most efficient ways to cook leaner cuts of meat, such as pork escalopes or beef or lamb steaks.

### DO . . .

***Preheat*** the frying pan, griddle or wok until very hot before adding the meat.

***Add a little fat*** to prevent the meat from sticking. You can either rub the fat on the meat to coat it, or add a little to the pan itself.

*Fry over a high heat* This sears the meat and seals in any juices; the more quickly the meat cooks, the less moisture it will lose.

*Use a ridged griddle pan* if you want to impart a slightly charred, smoky flavour to a steak.

DON'T . . .

*Rush it to the table* A steak should be allowed to rest for at least 5 minutes to ensure it is tender and juicy. Pour any juices from the rested meat back over the meat or use as the base for a sauce.

*Be tempted to move the meat around* in the pan if cooking a steak. Allow the steak to cook on one side for the desired length of time before turning it over; don't turn it over any sooner.

STIR-FRYING

This is best suited to Asian-inspired dishes where lean meat is cut into bite-sized pieces or strips and cooked very quickly and evenly. As with frying, it's important to preheat your wok or frying pan.

GRILLING

Grilling is one of the healthiest methods of cooking meat as it usually doesn't require any additional fat and also allows any fat within the meat to run out during cooking. It is often the preferred method for cooking pork and lamb chops. The heat source is from above only, so the meat will need to be turned halfway through cooking.

DO . . .

*Preheat the grill* at least 10 minutes ahead of cooking to ensure the meat will cook quickly.

DON'T . . .

*Leave a grill unattended* Grill temperatures vary and the cooking time will also be affected by the thickness of the meat you are using and the distance between the meat and the grill. The meat may need turning earlier than stated in a recipe, as these timings can only be approximate.

# SWEET SMOKED PAPRIKA LAMB WITH BORLOTTI BEANS

Cooked in one pot and serving a good number of people, this makes a great dish for a family gathering. You'll need to buy sliced chorizo, rather than chunky cubes, for this recipe.

Serves 6–8

PREPARE AHEAD
The lamb can be cooked up to 2 days ahead, the beans added when reheating.

FREEZE
Freezes well.

2 tbsp oil

1kg (2lb 3oz) diced lamb (from a leg of lamb)

175g (6oz) sliced chorizo, cut into small pieces

2 red onions, sliced

2 garlic cloves, crushed

1 aubergine, cut into 4cm (1½in) cubes

2 tsp sweet smoked paprika (see tip)

150ml (5fl oz) white wine

2 x 400g tins of chopped tomatoes

1 tbsp light muscovado sugar

1 x 400g tin of borlotti beans, drained and rinsed

salt and freshly ground black pepper

**1** Preheat the oven to 160°C/140°C fan/Gas 3.

**2** Heat the oil in a large, deep ovenproof frying pan or casserole dish. Add the diced lamb and fry over a high heat until browned all over – you will need to do this in batches. Remove the browned meat with a slotted spoon, place on a plate and set aside.

**3** Add the chorizo and cook until browned and crisp, then remove with the slotted spoon and add to the lamb. Tip in the onions and garlic and fry for about 3–4 minutes. Add the aubergine and fry for another 2 minutes. Sprinkle in the paprika, stir to coat the vegetables and fry for a further 2 minutes.

**4** Pour in the wine and tinned tomatoes and add the sugar. Return the browned lamb and chorizo to the pan, season with salt and pepper and bring to the boil, stirring. Cover the pan with a lid and transfer to the oven to cook for about an hour.

**5** Remove the pan from the oven and stir in the drained beans. Bring back up to the boil on the hob, cover again with the lid and return to the oven to cook for a further 30 minutes or until the lamb is tender. Serve immediately with a green vegetable.

## MARY'S FOOLPROOF TIPS

It's important to use sweet smoked paprika, rather than the hot smoked variety, which is more like chilli pepper and will make the dish very hot!

If you want to make a more generous serving, simply add another tin of borlotti beans.

# LAMB BURGERS WITH MINT MAYO AND TOMATO RELISH

These tasty burgers are perfect for a barbecue or al fresco eating. The tomato relish goes well with any grilled meat, in fact – from steaks and chops to bangers.

## FOR THE BURGERS
50g (2oz) fresh white breadcrumbs

1 garlic clove, crushed

1 small bunch of coriander, chopped

1½ tsp mint sauce

1 large red onion, roughly chopped

500g (1lb 2oz) lean minced lamb

1 tbsp olive oil, for frying

salt and freshly ground black pepper

8 brioche buns, to serve

3 cucumber dill pickle spears or gherkins, thinly sliced, to serve

## FOR THE RELISH
1 tbsp olive oil

1 onion, roughly chopped

1 garlic clove, crushed

1 x 400g tin of chopped tomatoes

1 tbsp balsamic vinegar

1 tbsp Worcestershire sauce

1 tbsp tomato ketchup

a pinch of sugar

## FOR THE MAYO
2 tbsp mayonnaise

2 tsp chopped mint

1 tsp mint sauce

Makes 8 burgers

**PREPARE AHEAD**
The raw burgers can be made up to 2 days ahead and cooked to order.

**FREEZE**
The burgers freeze well raw.

**1** Place the breadcrumbs, garlic, coriander, mint sauce and onion in a food processor. Season with salt and pepper and whizz until just combined and a fairly coarse texture. Tip into a bowl, add the minced lamb and mix together (see tip). Using wet hands (see tip), shape into eight burgers, then place on a tray and chill in the fridge until needed.

**2** Next make the tomato relish. Heat the oil in a saucepan, add the onion and garlic, then cover with a lid and fry over a medium heat for 5–7 minutes or until soft. Add all the remaining ingredients to the pan, bring to the boil and cook for 2–3 minutes. Season with salt and pepper, then cover again with the lid, reduce the heat and leave to simmer for about 10 minutes.

**3** To make the mint mayo, mix all the ingredients together in a small bowl.

**4** To cook the burgers, heat the oil in a large, non-stick frying pan or light the barbecue. Fry or barbecue the burgers for about 3–4 minutes on each side or until browned and cooked through.

**5** To serve, slice the buns in half and toast them. Spread one half of each bun with the tomato relish and add a lettuce leaf, a burger, a dollop of mint mayonnaise and a few slices of cucumber dill pickle before popping on the top half of the bun.

## MARY'S FOOLPROOF TIPS

Once the minced lamb is mixed with the other burger ingredients and seasoning, fry a small spoonful so that you can taste and adjust the seasoning as needed.

Wet hands help to shape the burgers, so it is easier to keep them all the same size.

# MADEIRA LAMB KIDNEYS

An old-fashioned dish but really delicious with its creamy blend of rich flavours and soft textures.
Ideal for a quick midweek supper as it's best made and served immediately. Lamb kidneys
are surprisingly inexpensive.

Serves 6

12 lamb's kidneys
(750g/1lb 10oz)

2 tbsp plain flour

3 tbsp sunflower oil

50g (2oz) butter

1 large onion, chopped

250g (9oz) button
mushrooms, sliced

100ml (3½fl oz)
Madeira or sherry

150ml (5fl oz)
double cream

2 tsp Dijon mustard

salt and freshly ground
black pepper

1 tbsp chopped
parsley, to serve

**1** Slice each kidney in half and remove the core (see tip). Place in a bowl, season with salt and pepper and sprinkle over the flour, then toss to coat.

**2** Heat the oil in a large frying pan, add the kidneys and cook over a high heat, turning occasionally, until browned all over (see tip). Remove with a slotted spoon and transfer to a plate.

**3** Melt the butter in the pan (no need to wash), add the onion and fry over a high heat for 3–4 minutes. Tip in the mushrooms and fry for 5–6 minutes, then remove with the slotted spoon and add to the plate with the kidneys.

**4** Pour in the Madeira and any juices that have collected on the kidney plate. Bring the mixture to the boil to reduce it by half, stirring with a wooden spoon as the liquid boils and scraping up any caramelised juices from the base of the pan.

**5** Add the cream and stir in the mustard. Bring back up to the boil and cook for 2 minutes, then return the mushrooms and kidneys to the pan, cover with a lid and simmer for 10 minutes until the kidneys are cooked through and tender.

**6** Serve hot, sprinkled with the chopped parsley and accompanied by rice.

## MARY'S FOOLPROOF TIPS

Kidneys can be slippery to handle. To remove the core easily, take a firm hold of the white membrane, and use kitchen scissors to snip out the cortex.

You may need to fry the kidneys in batches to ensure they are browned all over – a crowded pan would prevent them from browning.

# SLOW-ROAST SHOULDER OF LAMB WITH FLAGEOLET BEANS

This succulent roast has a French twist to it, inspired by my friend and assistant Lucy's recent trip to the village of St. Martin on holiday. Flageolet beans are the small, tender green beans often used in the rustic cooking of this part of the world.

Serves 6

PREPARE AHEAD
The lamb can be cooked up to 2 days ahead if serving cold.

1 large shoulder
of lamb

7 garlic cloves

500g (1lb 2oz) banana
shallots, peeled and
cut into wedges

4 celery sticks, sliced

1 tbsp oil

150ml (5fl oz)
white wine

200ml (7fl oz) strong
beef stock

2 x 400g tins of
flageolet beans,
drained and rinsed

1½ tbsp plain flour

a little gravy browning
(optional)

salt and freshly ground
black pepper

1 tbsp finely chopped
parsley, to serve

1 Preheat the oven to 220°C/200°C fan/Gas 7.

2 Sit the lamb, skin side up, on a board. Peel three of the garlic cloves and cut into slices. Using a sharp knife, pierce the skin at irregular intervals across the meat and insert slivers of garlic into each hole.

3 Peel and roughly chop the remaining garlic and add to a small roasting tin with the shallot wedges and celery, then place the lamb upside down on top of the vegetables. Drizzle with the oil.

4 Roast in oven for about 20 minutes until brown. Carefully turn the lamb over (so that it's skin side up) and roast for a further 20–30 minutes until browned all over.

5 Pour the wine and stock into the roasting tin and cover the lamb with foil. Reduce the oven temperature to 160°C/140°C fan/Gas 3 and slow-cook for about 3–3½ hours or until the lamb is completely tender (see tip overleaf). Transfer the lamb to a board and strain the cooking juices from the roasting tin into a measuring jug (reserve the vegetables in the tin). Remove some of the fat, then add a little more water to the jug to give you 600ml (1 pint) of liquid, and set aside.

6 Add the beans to the roasting tin and mix with the cooked vegetables, seasoning with salt and pepper. Sit the lamb back on top of the vegetables, uncovered, and return to the oven for a further 30 minutes until piping hot. Transfer the cooked meat to a board, cover with foil, and rest for 10 minutes while you make the gravy.

*Continues overleaf*

## SLOW-ROAST SHOULDER OF LAMB
## WITH FLAGEOLET BEANS *Continued*

**7** Measure the flour into a cup, add a little of the cooled liquid from the jug and mix into a smooth paste. Pour the rest of the liquid into a saucepan and add the flour paste. Whisk by hand over a high heat, until the gravy is thickened and bubbling. Check the seasoning, and add a little gravy browning, if you like, to make a darker gravy.

**8** Carve and shred the lamb and serve with the gravy and the vegetables and beans, sprinkled with the parsley.

........................................................................................

### MARY'S FOOLPROOF TIP

This is all about slow-cooking the lamb: if yours needs a little longer in the oven, it will not come to any harm. Or indeed, if someone is late for the meal, you don't need to worry – it will wait!

........................................................................................

# BUTTERFLIED LEG OF LAMB WITH PRESERVED LEMONS

You can buy a butterflied joint from your butcher. A 'butterflied' joint is where the bone has been removed and the meat opened out into roughly the shape of a butterfly. Making the meat flatter means it is quicker to cook – you could put it on a barbecue, for instance – and easier to carve. Great for serving a crowd, this would be delicious with broccoli and mash or saffron rice.

Serves 6–8

**PREPARE AHEAD**
The lamb can be marinated up to a day ahead.
The dressing can be made several hours ahead.

**FREEZE**
The raw, marinated lamb freezes well.

2.5kg (5½lb) leg of lamb, butterflied and the skin scored

FOR THE MARINADE

4 tbsp chopped thyme leaves

2 preserved lemons, chopped and pips discarded (see tip)

1 tbsp drained capers, chopped

4 garlic cloves, crushed

4 tbsp olive oil

1 tbsp runny honey

FOR THE
LEMON DRESSING

2 tbsp chopped thyme leaves

1 garlic clove, crushed

2 preserved lemons, finely chopped and pips discarded

6 tbsp olive oil

4 heaped tbsp chopped parsley

1 tbsp runny honey

salt and freshly ground black pepper

**1** Lay the lamb, skin side up, in a shallow dish. Mix all the marinade ingredients together in a bowl and pour over the lamb, massaging it in with your fingers, then leave to marinate in the fridge for 2–3 hours, or up to 12 hours ahead, if time allows.

**2** Preheat the oven to 220°C/200°C fan/Gas 7.

**3** Put the lamb, skin side up, in a roasting tin and pour over any marinade left in the dish. Roast in the oven for 30–35 minutes until dark golden and crisp on top and medium pink in the middle. Rest, covered in foil, for 10 minutes while you make the dressing.

**4** Measure all the dressing ingredients into a bowl and season with salt and pepper.

**5** Carve the lamb into slices and serve hot with the lemon dressing and juices from the roasting tin.

## MARY'S FOOLPROOF TIP

Preserved lemons are whole lemons that have been preserved by being packed into tall jars with salt, herbs and spices, then covered with lemon juice or brine and left to cure for a few weeks. They are used a lot in North African cooking, including tagines. It's best not to use too many, however, or they can overpower a dish.

# PASTA
# & RICE

# EXPRESS BACON AND PESTO PASTA

Full of delicious textures and flavours, this dish is ideal for a weekday lunch or supper as it's so quick to make. It is also excellent served as a cold pasta salad with the addition of a few tablespoons of good mayonnaise.

Serves 4–6

PREPARE AHEAD
Once made, keep covered in the fridge for up to 2 days.

1 x 150g (5oz) head of broccoli

1 onion, roughly chopped

350g (12oz) penne

300g (11oz) smoked back bacon, cut into small pieces

150g (5oz) fresh basil pesto

150g (5oz) cherry tomatoes, halved

25g (1oz) pine nuts, toasted (see tip on page 237)

25g (1oz) Parmesan cheese shavings

salt and freshly ground black pepper

1 Chop off the end of the woody stem from the head of broccoli and discard, then cut the broccoli into florets and chop the thinner green stems into small chunks.

2 Bring a pan of salted water to the boil and add the onion and penne (see tip). Cook the pasta according to the packet instructions, adding the broccoli florets and pieces of stem 3 minutes before the end of cooking. Drain the pasta and vegetables, then refresh the broccoli separately in cold water to stop the cooking and to set the colour.

3 While the pasta and vegetables are cooking, fry the bacon in a large, non-stick pan (no oil added) over a medium-high heat for about 10 minutes, stirring frequently, until crispy and golden all over. Spoon out about 2 tablespoons of the cooked bacon and set aside.

4 Remove any excess fat from the pan, retaining the remaining bacon. Add the pesto and tomatoes with the cooked pasta, onion and broccoli, season with pepper and stir to combine.

5 Tip into a serving dish, scatter with toasted pine nuts, the reserved bacon and the shavings of Parmesan and serve.

## MARY'S FOOLPROOF TIPS

Cooking the onion with the pasta makes sure it is tender and soft.

Be aware that if you serve the day after making, the broccoli will have lost some of its colour, though it will still be delicious.

# BAKED MACARONI CHEESE WITH TOMATOES

**This is one for the children, though secretly all the grown-ups love it too!
Serve for lunch or supper with a green salad or peas.**

Serves 6

PREPARE AHEAD
Can be assembled up to 12 hours ahead.

275g (10oz) macaroni
50g (2oz) butter
50g (2oz) plain flour
1 litre (1¾ pints) hot
  milk
1½ tbsp Dijon mustard
150g (5oz)
  extra-mature Cheddar
  cheese, grated
4 large tomatoes,
  halved and sliced
salt and freshly ground
  black pepper

1 You will need a 1.75-litre (3-pint) ovenproof dish. Preheat the oven to 200°C/180°C fan/Gas 6.

2 Bring a pan of salted water to the boil, add the macaroni and cook according to the packet instructions or until al dente (just undercooked). Drain and refresh in cold water.

3 To make the cheese sauce, melt the butter in a saucepan, add the flour and whisk over a high heat for 30 seconds. Gradually whisk in the hot milk (see tip) over a high heat, then bring to the boil and cook for 2 minutes until thickened and smooth.

4 Remove from the heat, add the mustard and two-thirds of the cheese and season well with salt and pepper.

5 Add the cooked macaroni to the sauce, stir to combine and then pour into the ovenproof dish. Arrange the tomato slices, slightly overlapping, on top and push down slightly into the sauce. Sprinkle with the remaining cheese.

6 Bake in the oven for 25–30 minutes until golden, piping hot and bubbling. Serve straight from the oven.

## MARY'S FOOLPROOF TIP

Adding hot milk enables the roux (butter and flour mixture) to absorb the milk quickly and the sauce to come to the boil more rapidly, making it less likely to be lumpy. Semi-skimmed or full-fat milk doesn't matter – use whatever you have in the fridge.

# GARDEN TAGLIATELLE

Here pasta is mixed with fresh vegetables in a flavoursome tomato sauce to make a sustaining but healthy dish. It is perfect for using up a glut of homegrown courgettes or tomatoes, and you could swap in other vegetables too, if you liked.

Serves 6

PREPARE AHEAD
The tomato sauce can be made up to a day ahead; the rest of the dish then cooked when you're ready to serve.

350g (12oz) tagliatelle

2 tbsp olive oil

350g (12oz) mixed yellow and green courgettes, sliced

200g (7oz) button mushrooms, sliced

50g (2oz) Parmesan cheese, finely grated, to serve

FOR THE TOMATO SAUCE

2 tbsp olive oil

1 large onion, chopped

3 garlic cloves, crushed

2 x 400g tins of chopped tomatoes

4 ripe tomatoes, chopped

a pinch of sugar

1 small bunch of basil, chopped, plus a few leaves to garnish

salt and freshly ground black pepper

1 First make the tomato sauce. Heat the oil in a large saucepan, add the onion and garlic and fry over a medium-high heat for about 5 minutes. Add the tinned and the fresh tomatoes and season with the sugar and some salt and pepper. Bring to the boil, stirring, then lower the heat and simmer for 20 minutes until reduced and thickened slightly. Add the chopped basil.

2 Meanwhile, bring a pan of salted water to the boil and cook the tagliatelle according to the packet instructions, then drain.

3 While the pasta is cooking, heat the oil in a large frying pan, add the courgettes and fry on both sides over a medium-high heat for 6–8 minutes or until golden (you may need to do this in batches). Remove with a slotted spoon and set aside. Add the mushrooms to the pan, with a little extra oil if needed, and fry for 5–6 minutes until golden brown, then remove from the pan and add to the fried courgettes.

4 Tip the drained pasta into the pan of tomato sauce, followed by the courgettes and mushrooms. Toss everything together, season to taste (see tip) and turn into a serving dish. Serve sprinkled with Parmesan and the remaining basil.

## MARY'S FOOLPROOF TIP

Remember to taste the sauce and add sugar and extra salt and pepper, if needed, to balance out the flavours before serving.

# TUNA AND SPINACH LINGUINE

Full of flavour from the spinach, tuna and cherry tomatoes, this recipe is very healthy too.
Not a drop of cream anywhere! This dish is so lovely and fresh – it is best made and eaten immediately.
Great to knock up for a midweek supper.

Serves 6

PREPARE AHEAD
The pasta can be cooked ahead, drained and refreshed in cold water up to 4 hours
before cooking the rest of the dish.

350g (12oz) linguine

2 x 200g tins of tuna
in olive oil, drained
and oil reserved

2 garlic cloves, crushed

4 tinned or bottled
anchovy fillets,
finely chopped

2 large shallots,
finely chopped

1 fresh red chilli,
deseeded and
finely chopped

2 tbsp drained
baby capers

12 cherry tomatoes,
halved

225g (8oz) baby
spinach leaves,
coarsely shredded

salt and freshly ground
black pepper

TO SERVE

finely grated zest and
juice of 1 small lemon

2 tbsp finely grated
Parmesan cheese

1 Bring a large pan of salted water to the boil, add the linguine and cook
according to the packet instructions, then drain.

2 Meanwhile, measure 2 tablespoons of oil reserved from the tuna tins into a
large frying or sauté pan. Add the garlic, anchovies, shallots and chilli and fry
over a high heat for 5–6 minutes until the shallots have softened. Add the capers,
cherry tomatoes and spinach leaves and toss until the spinach is just wilting.

3 Tip the drained linguine and the flaked tuna into the pan. Season with a little
salt and pepper and carefully toss together until combined (see tip), adding more
oil if the mixture seems too dry.

4 Tip into a serving bowl and sprinkle with the lemon zest and juice and
grated Parmesan to serve.

## MARY'S FOOLPROOF TIP

You have to be quick with the frying and tossing together or the pasta will break
up and everything will stick together!

# FOOLPROOF PASTA & RICE

Both excellent store-cupboard staples, pasta and rice have become essential ingredients in our everyday cooking, enabling us to whip up speedy midweek meals as well as more indulgent, comforting family suppers for the weekend. Although they are relatively straightforward to cook, these tips and tricks should help you get good results every time.

PASTA

DO . . .

*Buy the best-quality pasta you can afford* The best Italian pastas are made from 100% durum wheat.

*Use a large pan and plenty of water* Pasta needs space to ensure it cooks evenly.

*Add a generous amount of salt* to the cooking water. It's important to get the most flavour from the pasta.

*Ensure the water is rapidly boiling* before adding the pasta.

*Check the pasta is cooked before draining it* Remove a piece of pasta using a slotted spoon and carefully bite into it; the pasta should be tender but with a little resistance rather than soft all the way through – the Italians call this 'al dente' (tender but firm to the bite).

*Undercook pasta for pasta bakes* It is best to undercook pasta slightly if it is going to be used in a pasta bake and therefore cooked for a second time. If you just parboil the pasta initially, this will prevent it from overcooking in the oven.

*Retain a little of the pasta cooking water* to loosen the sauce, if necessary.

DON'T . . .

*Forget to check the packet instructions* Cooking times for different types of pasta vary, with fresh varieties cooking much more quickly than dried.

*Allow the pasta to sit* once drained or it will dry out and become sticky and overcooked. It's best to ensure your sauce is going to be ready as soon as the pasta is cooked so that you can combine them straight away. If the pasta has dried out, plunge it into boiling salted water and leave for 1 minute to separate the shapes or strands, then drain it and serve at once.

PASTA SHAPES

When cooking during the week, it's easy to reach for whatever pasta shape is in the cupboard, but if you really want to achieve the perfect pasta dish, it's important to follow a few simple rules when it comes to matching pasta shapes with sauces. Different shapes lend themselves to different sauces, whether chunky or smooth, thick or thin, rich or light.

| PASTA SHAPE | EXAMPLE | EXAMPLE |
| --- | --- | --- |
| Long strands | Spaghetti or linguine | Smooth or light sauces or those with little bits in them, e.g. seafood or olive oil-based sauces (e.g. chilli, garlic, parsley and olive oil) |
| Ribbon-like pasta | Tagliatelle or pappardelle | Meaty or rich sauces, e.g. meat ragout or carbonara |
| Short, chunky shapes | Rigatoni or penne | Chunky sauces, often those made with vegetables, e.g. pasta alla Norma (with aubergines and tomatoes) |
| Mini pasta | Orzo or fregola | Best added to soups or casseroles |
| Twists | Fusilli or trofie | Light sauces like pesto |

## RICE

### TYPES OF RICE

*Long-grain rice* There are many varieties of this commonly used rice. I use par-boiled American rice which is easy to cook and has a translucent yellow colour. Basmati is one of the best for producing separate, fluffy grains when cooked.

*Wholegrain or brown rice* The bran layer and germ of the rice are left intact so that it is more fibrous and nutritious. It means that it takes longer to cook – usually about 25 minutes.

*Short-grain rice* This kind of rice includes Italian risotto rice, of which there are three main varieties: Arborio, carnaroli and vialone nano. Risotto rice needs to be cooked in an entirely different way to long-grain rice. In fact, it is almost the opposite in technique. Here the starch in the rice is needed to give the risotto its trademark creamy, unctuous/velvety texture. When making a risotto, the stock is added gradually and the rice stirred constantly to encourage it to release more starch. It takes a bit of practice to get it right, but once you have mastered the skill, you will have it for life. Short-grain pudding rice is best for rice pudding.

*Wild rice* is not actually a rice, but a black seed from a grass that can be cooked and eaten in the same way as rice. It is often mixed with white or wholegrain rice to add flavour and texture to rice-based dishes. It takes longer to cook, however, so be sure to check the packet instructions.

## FOOLPROOF TIPS FOR PERFECT FLUFFY RICE

There are two ways of cooking long-grain rice to achieve a light and fluffy result:

**The open pan method** Here rice is cooked in a large pan of rapidly boiling water. Add the rice only when the water is boiling rapidly, then boil for about 2 minutes less than the recommended time. Drain the rice and return to the hot pan, cover with a tight-fitting lid and set aside, off the heat, for 3–4 minutes. The rice should have finished cooking in the residual heat and the grains should be tender and fluffy.

**The absorption method** This is where the rice is cooked in a measured amount of water in a covered pan over a low heat. The rice absorbs all the water as it cooks before being set aside for a few minutes to finish cooking in the steam. The general ratio is double the amount of water to rice, but this varies according to the recipe and depends on the texture desired.

### DO . . .

**Rinse basmati and other long-grain rice** under cold water until the water runs clear before cooking. This helps remove some of the starch, which can make rice stodgy or gluey.

### DON'T . . .

**Use a spoon** to stir long-grain rice. Always use a fork, as this helps prevent the rice grains from breaking, which can cause them to stick together.

## FOOLPROOF TIPS FOR PERFECT RISOTTO

### DO . . .

**Have patience** The stock needs to be added in stages, allowing each ladleful to be absorbed before the next one is poured in.

**Ensure the stock remains hot** Keep it in a separate saucepan over a very low heat.

**Keep stirring** While it's tempting to think that the rice should cook on its own if you leave the pan to bubble for a few minutes, it's the constant stirring action that helps the starch to come out of the grains and creates the lovely creamy texture.

**Allow the risotto to rest at the end of cooking** When the rice is al dente (has a slight bite to it) and all the stock has been absorbed, remove the pan from the heat and stir in grated Parmesan or other cheese and a small knob of butter. Cover with a lid and set aside for a couple of minutes; this allows all the flavours to amalgamate and helps to achieve the perfect consistency.

### DON'T . . .

**Cook risotto in large quantities** (to serve more than eight). The technique is much easier to master if you are cooking for smaller numbers.

# CREAMY ROASTED PEPPER PASTA WITH FETA AND OLIVES

This tasty pasta dish is great for a quick supper. The red peppers are cooked from scratch here, but if you are really short of time, you could substitute with roasted peppers from a jar.

Serves 6

**PREPARE AHEAD**
The peppers can be roasted and the sauce made up to 8 hours ahead. Store the sauce in the fridge and assemble with the cooked pasta and other ingredients to serve. The finished dish can kept stored in the fridge for up to 1 day.

4 large red peppers, deseeded and cut into 2cm (¾in) chunks

2 tbsp olive oil

350g (12oz) penne

2 garlic cloves, halved

50g (2oz) Parmesan cheese, grated

4 tbsp chopped basil

½ fresh red chilli, deseeded and chopped

150ml (5fl oz) double cream

200g (7oz) feta cheese, broken into pieces

75g (3oz) black olives, pitted

juice of ½ small lemon

salt and freshly ground black pepper

**1** Preheat the oven to 220°C/200°C fan/Gas 7.

**2** Place the peppers on a baking tray, drizzle over the oil, season with salt and pepper and roast in the oven for 25–30 minutes or until soft and tinged brown. Set aside to cool.

**3** Bring a pan of salted water to the boil, add the penne and cook according to the packet instructions (see tip). Drain, reserving 100ml (3½fl oz) of the pasta water.

**4** Meanwhile, tip half the roasted peppers into a food processor with the garlic, Parmesan and half the basil. Add the chilli and cream, season with salt and pepper and whizz until smooth.

**5** Pour this sauce into a large saucepan and heat through on the hob until bubbling. Add the drained pasta with the feta, olives, lemon juice and remaining chopped basil and roasted peppers with any juices. Pour in the reserved pasta water, season with salt and pepper and carefully toss together.

**6** Spoon into a warmed dish and serve immediately.

## MARY'S FOOLPROOF TIP

Always cook the penne so it is al dente – with just a small bite to it; overdone pasta can split and ruin the dish.

# LEBANESE RICE SALAD

I love the different flavours in this salad – the subtle spices, sharp lemon and olives and the nutty brown and wild rice. Great for a party or to serve with grilled meat or fish.

Serves 6 as a side dish

PREPARE AHEAD
Can be made up to a day ahead and dressed up to 3 hours in advance, if kept in the fridge.

200g (7oz) brown rice

50g (2oz) wild rice

200g (7oz) baby broad beans (see tip)

3 celery sticks, very finely diced

6 spring onions, finely sliced

75g (3oz) green olives, pitted and sliced into thirds

1 bunch of flat-leaf parsley, chopped

1 tbsp chopped mint

salt and freshly ground black pepper

FOR THE DRESSING

finely grated zest and juice of 1 large lemon

2 garlic cloves, crushed

6 tbsp olive oil

2 tsp caster sugar

1 tsp ground cinnamon

1 tsp ground cumin

1 Cook each type of rice in separate pans of boiling salted water according to the packet instructions, then drain and refresh in cold water. Tip into a bowl and set aside.

2 Cook the broad beans in boiling salted water for 5 minutes, then drain and refresh in cold water (see tip on page 184) before adding to the rice.

3 Add the celery to the bowl with the spring onions, sliced olives and chopped herbs, season well with salt and pepper and toss together.

4 Mix all the dressing ingredients together in a small bowl, pour over the rice salad and mix well. Leave in the fridge for 3 hours before checking the seasoning, and serving.

## MARY'S FOOLPROOF TIP

Young baby broad beans are very tender with soft skins that do not need to be removed; frozen broad beans are the same. End-of-season fresh beans will need to be removed from their tough outer skins: after refreshing in cold water, simply squeeze the beans gently to pop them out of their skins before adding to the rice.

# SALMON, FENNEL AND PEA RISOTTO

**Risotto is such a quick and healthy supper dish: the creamy rice is complemented here by the salmon and peas. Be careful not to overcook it, though, or it will be stodgy.**

Serves 4–6

750ml (1 pint 6fl oz) hot fish or vegetable stock

2 tbsp sunflower oil

½ fennel bulb (or 1 small bulb), trimmed and finely chopped

2 garlic cloves, crushed

225g (8oz) Arborio or risotto rice

300ml (10fl oz) white wine

150g (5oz) frozen petits pois

juice of ½ lemon

2 salmon fillets (300g/11oz in total), skinned and thinly sliced

3 tbsp full-fat crème fraîche

3 sprigs of tarragon, coarsely chopped

30g (1oz) Parmesan cheese, grated, plus extra for sprinkling

salt and freshly ground black pepper

50g (2oz) pea shoots, to garnish

1 Pour the stock into a saucepan and keep warm over a low heat (see tip).

2 Pour the oil into a large frying pan over a medium-high heat, add the fennel and fry for about 4 minutes to soften (but not brown), stirring frequently. Add the garlic and rice and fry for a minute, stirring constantly, until each grain of rice is coated in the oil.

3 Pour the wine into the stock and stir, bring to a gentle simmer and then gradually begin adding the hot stock mixture, a ladleful at a time, to the rice mixture in the pan, stirring continuously, and waiting until the stock has been almost fully absorbed before adding the next ladleful. Cook the rice for 15–20 minutes, until you are left with about 250ml (9fl oz) of stock in the saucepan (about a quarter of the original quantity of liquid) and the rice is nearly cooked.

4 Add the petits pois and lemon juice. Ladle in some of the remaining stock and keep stirring for a couple of minutes. Add the salmon slices with the crème fraîche, tarragon and Parmesan and stir through.

5 Season to taste with salt and pepper and serve immediately (see tip), sprinkled with extra Parmesan and garnished with pea shoots.

## MARY'S FOOLPROOF TIPS

It is important to add the stock when it is hot. Adding cold stock means the mixture will take too long to boil and the rice will be overcooked.

It is important to serve as soon as it is cooked, as risottos do not keep well on the heat – they become soggy and the peas will lose their colour.

# JASMINE RICE WITH PRAWNS AND PAK CHOI

**Jasmine rice has a fragrant flavour and is often used in Thai cooking. The grain is long and pointed. This is a simple rice dish with subtle flavours that are offset by the firm, juicy texture of the prawns and pak choi.**

Serves 6

PREPARE AHEAD
The rice can be cooked up to 3 hours ahead and kept chilled in the fridge.

250g (9oz) jasmine rice

50g (2oz) butter

1 large onion, chopped

1 red pepper,
deseeded and diced

200g (7oz) button
mushrooms, sliced

1 large garlic
clove, crushed

4cm (1½in) knob of
fresh root ginger,
peeled and finely
grated (see tip on
page 187)

3 tablespoons
soy sauce

a dash of hot pepper
sauce such as Tabasco

1 tbsp light
muscovado sugar

1 tbsp sesame oil, plus
extra for frying

350g (12oz) raw,
peeled king prawns

juice of ½ lemon

250g (9oz) pak choi,
chopped into
large pieces

salt and freshly ground
black pepper

1 Cook the rice in boiling salted water according to the packet instructions, then drain and rinse under cold running water to cool down completely before leaving to stand in a large sieve in a cool place for 1 hour to dry out (see tip).

2 Melt half the butter in a large frying pan or wok over a high heat. Add the onion and fry, stirring regularly, for about 5 minutes until nearly soft but not browned. Increase the heat to high, add the red pepper with the mushrooms, garlic and ginger and fry for 3–4 minutes. Tip in the cooked rice and fry for a couple of minutes until the rice is hot.

3 Mix the soy sauce in a bowl with the Tabasco, sugar and sesame oil. Pour over the rice mixture and toss together over the heat, then set aside and keep warm in the pan.

4 Heat another frying pan until hot. Add the remaining butter, then fry the prawns on a high heat for 3–4 minutes until pink and cooked through. Squeeze over the lemon juice and season with salt and pepper before adding to the rice mixture.

5 Spoon the rice mixture into a hot serving dish. Heat a little extra oil in the second frying pan (no need to wash), add the pak choi and cook over a high heat for a minute until just wilted, then season with salt and pepper and arrange in a line along the middle of the rice mixture. Serve immediately.

## MARY'S FOOLPROOF TIP

The rice must be dry before adding to the frying pan – speedy cooking is important for this dish.

# SALADS & VEGETABLES

# SATURDAY LUNCH TUNA SALAD

**Full of colour and flavour, this is a substantial salad that can be served as a main dish. The ingredients look more attractive arranged on a platter than mixed in a bowl.**

Serves 6 as a main dish

PREPARE AHEAD
Assemble the main salad up to 4 hours ahead and dress to serve. The croutons can be made up to 5 days ahead.

250g (9oz) baby new potatoes (unpeeled)

200g (7oz) fine green beans

3 eggs

2 large avocados (see tip)

juice of ½ lemon

2 large Little Gem lettuces (see tip), cut into small wedges

250g (9oz) cherry tomatoes, halved

2 x 120g tins of tuna in oil

2 tbsp snipped chives

FOR THE CROUTONS

100g (4oz) white bread (stale is best)

2 tbsp olive oil

salt and freshly ground black pepper

FOR THE DRESSING

2 tbsp grainy mustard

3 tbsp white wine vinegar

juice of ½ lemon

8 tbsp olive oil

2 tbsp runny honey

1 First make the croutons. Slice the bread into 1–2cm (½–¾in) cubes, tip into a bowl or resealable freezer bag, add the oil, season with salt and pepper and toss together. Fry in a pan over a high heat until golden and crisp, then tip on to a plate lined with kitchen paper and set aside to cool.

2 For the dressing, measure all the ingredients into a bowl. Whisk until combined.

3 Cook the potatoes in boiling salted water for about 15 minutes or until tender. Drain, cut in half and tip into a bowl. Add half the dressing to the hot potatoes (see tip on page 186), season with salt and pepper and set aside to cool.

4 While the potatoes are boiling, cook the green beans in a separate pan of boiling salted water for 4 minutes. Drain and refresh in cold water (see tip on page 184) before cutting each bean in half.

5 To cook the eggs, place in another saucepan, cover with cold water, bring to the boil on a high heat and boil for 9 minutes, then drain and run under cold water. Peel and slice into quarters.

6 Peel each avocado and cut in half, removing the stone, then slice the flesh and mix with the lemon juice (see tip on page 25).

7 To assemble the salad, take a large platter and arrange the lettuce over the base. Scatter over the avocados, potatoes, beans, eggs and tomatoes. Drain the tuna, break into chunks and scatter over the salad with the croutons. Season with salt and pepper and pour over the dressing. Scatter with the chives to serve.

## MARY'S FOOLPROOF TIPS

The avocados should be firm but ripe – if they are overripe then they will turn to mush in the salad and be lost.

You could substitute the Little Gem with another firm lettuce, such as Tom Thumb.

# ORIENTAL VEGETABLE AND NOODLE SALAD WITH GINGER

*I adore this recipe – so light and fresh with all the healthy vegetables (see tip) and the extra-fine rice noodles. Instead of the crayfish, you could use prawns, sliced beef fillet or shredded chicken. You could also sprinkle over 30g (1oz) chopped salted peanuts just before serving, if you like.*

200g (7oz) extra-fine dried rice noodles

½ cucumber

150g (5oz) crayfish tails, cooked and peeled

1 red pepper, deseeded and finely sliced

150g (5oz) bean sprouts

6 spring onions, finely sliced on the diagonal

1 small carrot, peeled and cut into fine matchsticks

½–1 fresh red chilli, deseeded and finely chopped

1 small bunch of coriander, chopped

1 small bunch of mint, chopped (see tip)

3cm (1¼in) knob of fresh root ginger, peeled and finely grated (see tip on page 187)

1 garlic clove, crushed

salt and freshly ground black pepper

FOR THE DRESSING

3 tbsp Thai fish sauce

3 tbsp lime juice (1–2 limes)

3 tbsp light muscovado sugar

1 tbsp sesame oil

Serves 6 as a side dish or 4 as a main dish

PREPARE AHEAD
The vegetables can be prepared up to 6 hours ahead. Add the herbs and dress just before serving.

1 Cook the rice noodles in boiling water according to the packet instructions, or until they are slightly al dente, then drain and refresh in cold water. Drain again and snip into shorter lengths.

2 Cut the cucumber in half lengthways. Using a teaspoon, scoop out the seeds along the middle of each half and discard. Thinly slice the cucumber on the diagonal and tip into a large salad bowl.

3 Add all the remaining salad ingredients to the bowl, along with the cooked noodles, season with salt and pepper and toss together.

4 Mix all the ingredients for the dressing together in a separate bowl. Just before serving, pour over the dressing and toss everything together.

## MARY'S FOOLPROOF TIPS

Buy the freshest, finest, seasonal ingredients you can – this is all about raw flavour.

If you have no fresh mint, add a tablespoon of mint sauce from a jar instead.

# ROASTED VEGETABLE QUICHE

**Filled with colourful chunky vegetables and large enough to serve a crowd, this flan would make a decorative addition to a summer buffet. Roasting the vegetables, and including Gruyère with its distinctive flavour, ensures that it is very tasty too.**

Serves 10–12 as a main dish

PREPARE AHEAD
Once made, the quiche can be kept chilled in the fridge for 1–2 days. The pastry case can be made a day in advance and stored in an airtight container before filling.

FREEZE
The raw pastry freezes well, as does the cooked flan.

FOR THE PASTRY
225g (8oz) plain flour, plus extra for dusting
175g (6oz) cold butter, cubed
1 egg, beaten

FOR THE FILLING
2 onions
2 red peppers
200g (7oz) baby courgettes
1–2 tbsp olive oil
300ml (10fl oz) double cream
4 eggs
180g (6oz) Gruyère cheese, grated
salt and freshly ground black pepper

1 You will need a 28cm (11in) round, loose-bottomed fluted tart tin and some baking beans.

2 First make the pastry. Blitz the flour and butter in a food processor (or place in a mixing bowl and rub the butter into the flour with your fingertips). Once combined, add the egg and 1 tablespoon of cold water and pulse until combined.

3 Roll out the dough on a lightly floured, cold work surface a circle large enough to line the tart tin and about 3mm (⅛in) thick, leaving a generous edge to allow for shrinking in the oven (see tip on page 262). Prick the base and sides of the pastry in the tin and chill in the fridge for 15 minutes. While the case is chilling, preheat the oven to 180°C/160°C fan/Gas 4.

4 Line the chilled pastry with baking paper, fill with baking beans and bake in the oven for 10 minutes. Remove the beans and paper and put the pastry case back in the oven to bake for another 10–15 minutes. Remove from the oven and set aside to cool (see tip overleaf). Increase the oven temperature to 200°C/180°C fan/ Gas 6 and start preparing the vegetables.

5 Peel and quarter both onions, then halve each quarter lengthways. Deseed and cut the peppers into chunky strips and halve the courgettes lengthways. Place on a large baking tray, drizzle with olive oil and season generously with salt and pepper. Roast in the oven for 30–40 minutes, turning the vegetables over halfway through cooking, until tender and golden.

*Continues overleaf*

# ROASTED VEGETABLE QUICHE *Continued*

6 Meanwhile, whisk together the cream, eggs and half the grated cheese and season well with salt and pepper. Once the vegetables are roasted, sprinkle the remaining cheese on to the base of the pastry case, pile in the vegetables – spreading them out so that they are evenly distributed – and pour over the cream mixture.

7 Reduce the oven temperature back down to 180°C/160°C/Gas 4 and bake the quiche for 25–35 minutes or until the filling is set and golden on top. Take out of the oven and allow to cool slightly before removing from the tin (see tip on page 246) and transferring to a serving plate. Serve warm.

## MARY'S FOOLPROOF TIP

If there are any cracks in the pastry after blind-baking, use a little leftover raw dough to fill them in. Press the dough into the cracks and seal with a little of the egg mixture, working it in well, before filling with the cheese, vegetables and egg mixture, so the filling doesn't leak out during baking.

# MIDDLE EASTERN AUBERGINE AND CHICKPEA SALAD

**This is a different sort of salad, full of flavour from the za'atar blend (which I've also used in a marinade for chicken – see page 84) and with lovely contrasting textures. (Pictured overleaf.)**

Serves 6 as a side dish or 4 as a main dish

PREPARE AHEAD
Can be made up to 4 hours ahead. The yoghurt dip tastes even better if made the day before.

3 aubergines

3 tbsp olive oil

1½ tbsp za'atar spice blend

250g (9oz) cherry tomatoes, halved

1 x 400g tin of chickpeas, drained and rinsed

salt and freshly ground black pepper

FOR THE DRESSING

4 tbsp olive oil

juice of ½ lemon

1 garlic clove, crushed

2 tbsp chopped parsley

2 tbsp chopped mint

a pinch of sugar

FOR THE YOGHURT DIP

150g (5oz) natural Greek yoghurt

2 tbsp chopped mint

1 Preheat the oven to 220°C/200°C fan/Gas 6.

2 Cut each aubergine into five slices lengthways, then cut each slice in half lengthways to make long thin strips.

3 Arrange the aubergine slices on a large baking tray (you may need two trays) in a single layer (see tip). Drizzle over the oil, sprinkle with 1 tablespoon of the za'atar and season with salt and pepper.

4 Roast in the oven for 20–25 minutes until golden brown and tender. Remove from the tray and set aside to cool.

5 Place the tomatoes, cut side up, on the hot baking tray. Sprinkle with the remaining ½ tablespoon of za'atar and season with salt and pepper. Slide the tray into the oven and then switch it off, leaving the tomatoes for about 8 minutes to soften slightly in the residual heat. Remove from the oven and set aside to cool.

6 Measure all the dressing ingredients into a large bowl and whisk to combine. Remove 1 tablespoon of the dressing to use for serving, then add the drained chickpeas to the bowl, season with salt and pepper and toss to combine.

7 For the dip, add the yoghurt and mint to a small bowl and season with salt and pepper.

8 Spread the aubergine slices on a large platter, spoon over the dressed chickpeas and arrange the softened tomatoes on top. Drizzle over the remaining dressing and serve with a dollop of yoghurt dip.

## MARY'S FOOLPROOF TIP

To prevent the aubergines from sweating rather than roasting, the oven needs to be hot and the aubergine strips must lie in a single layer on the baking tray.

# BROAD BEAN, PEA AND ASPARAGUS SALAD WITH MINT DRESSING

This salad tastes of summer – lots of lovely fresh green vegetables offset by the mint dressing. It would be great for a barbecue or al fresco meal. Do not assemble the dish more than 2 hours ahead, as the beans and asparagus will lose their colour on standing.

Serves 6 as a side dish

PREPARE AHEAD
The vegetables can be cooked and refreshed up to 6 hours ahead and dressed to serve. The dressing can be made a day in advance, omitting the chopped mint until serving. The dish must be assembled no more than 2 hours ahead.

300g (11oz) asparagus spears

300g (11oz) fresh podded peas or frozen petit pois

300g (11oz) fresh podded broad beans or frozen baby broad beans

salt and freshly ground black pepper

FOR THE MINT DRESSING

6 tbsp olive oil

3 tbsp white wine vinegar

1 tsp Dijon mustard

2 tsp caster sugar

2 heaped tbsp chopped mint

1 Put a large pan of salted water on to boil. Cut or snap off the woody ends of the asparagus spears and slice each of the stems on the diagonal into 2cm (¾in) pieces, leaving a 3cm (1¼in) tip.

2 Add the peas and beans to the boiling water and return to the boil for 2 minutes. Keeping the heat turned up high, add the chopped asparagus stems and boil for 1 minute. Then add the asparagus tips and boil for another minute. Drain all the vegetables in a colander and refresh in cold water (see tip) before tipping into a serving bowl.

3 To make the dressing, mix all the ingredients together to combine. Season the vegetables with salt and pepper and toss in the dressing to serve.

## MARY'S FOOLPROOF TIPS

It is vital to refresh the vegetables in cold water; this stops them from cooking further and sets their bright green colour.

# WARM BROCCOLI AND TOMATO SALAD

**With its fresh flavours and contrasting textures, this salad would be perfect with barbecued or cold meats.**

Serves 6 as a side dish

PREPARE AHEAD
The salad (including the broccoli) can be prepared up to 6 hours ahead and then the potatoes cooked to serve.

350g (12oz) baby new potatoes (unpeeled)

450g (1lb) tenderstem broccoli

175g (6oz) sun-blushed tomatoes, drained (if in oil) and cut in half

3 tbsp chopped parsley

3 tbsp drained capers, roughly chopped

salt and freshly ground black pepper

FOR THE DRESSING

1 tbsp Dijon mustard

2 tbsp white wine vinegar

6 tbsp olive oil

1 tsp caster sugar

1 garlic clove, crushed

1 Place the potatoes in a saucepan of salted water. Bring to the boil and boil for 10–12 minutes until just cooked and tender, then drain.

2 Meanwhile, cut the woody end of the stems from the broccoli, then cut each stem of broccoli into three. Cook the broccoli in boiling salted water for 5 minutes until tender but still with a little bite, then drain and refresh in cold water (see tip on page 184). Slice the cooked potatoes in half and place in a bowl.

3 Mix all the dressing ingredients together in a separate small bowl and whisk to combine. Pour 3 tablespoons of the dressing over the warm potatoes (see tip) and season with salt and pepper.

4 Arrange the broccoli on a large platter, scatter over the dressed potatoes and halved tomatoes. Sprinkle with the parsley and scatter over the capers, then drizzle over the remaining dressing just before serving.

## MARY'S FOOLPROOF TIP

Pour the dressing over the potatoes while they are still warm, so that the flavour soaks in.

# SAVOY CABBAGE STIR-FRY WITH GINGER

**Fresh and light and very quick to make, this simple stir-fry would go well with chops or fish fillets.**

Serves 6 as a side dish

PREPARE AHEAD
Boil the cabbage, refresh in cold water and leave to drain for up to 6 hours ahead.
Stir-fry to serve.

1 savoy cabbage,
   core removed and
   leaves shredded

25g (1oz) butter

2cm (¾in) knob of
   fresh root ginger,
   peeled and finely
   grated (see tip)

salt and freshly ground
   black pepper

1 Cook the cabbage in a large pan of boiling salted water for 3 minutes, then drain.

2 Melt the butter in a large frying pan, add the ginger and fry for a few seconds. Add the cooked cabbage and stir-fry over a high heat, seasoning with salt and pepper and tossing until piping hot.

3 Tip into a serving dish and serve.

## MARY'S FOOLPROOF TIP

Peel the ginger with a sharp knife or, if the root is very young, you can simply rub off the skin. Any spare ginger can be wrapped in cling film and frozen or kept in the fridge, if not needed.

# RED LENTILS WITH CHILLI AND GINGER

Made in a similar way to a risotto, with the stock being added a little at a time, this is perfect for serving with meat or fish, such as the Spiced, Blackened Salmon on page 62. Increase the chilli if you like things hot.

Serves 6 as a side dish

1 tbsp oil

3 garlic cloves, crushed

5cm (2in) knob of fresh root ginger, peeled and finely grated (see tip on page 187)

1 fresh red chilli, deseeded and finely chopped

1 tbsp ground cumin

500g (1lb 2oz) dried red lentils

1.1 litres (2 pints) vegetable or chicken stock

1 tbsp chopped coriander

1 tbsp chopped mint

salt and freshly ground black pepper

1 Heat the oil in a large frying pan, add the garlic, ginger and chilli and fry over a high heat for 3–4 minutes. Sprinkle in the cumin and fry for a further 30 seconds.

2 Add the lentils, stirring to coat in the oil and spices, then (still over a high heat) gradually ladle in the stock, stirring constantly and allowing the liquid to be absorbed between additions, until all the liquid has been incorporated and the lentils are tender (about 20 minutes, or according to packet instructions). The mixture should be creamy and loose in consistency, not stodgy.

3 Season with salt and pepper (see tip), scatter with the chopped coriander and mint and serve hot.

## MARY'S FOOLPROOF TIP

Do not add salt to the dish any earlier as it can toughen the skins of the dried lentils so that they don't soften during cooking.

# HASSELBACK POTATOES

Named after the fancy Hasselbacken hotel and restaurant in Stockholm, from which the dish originated, these make a delicious alternative to roast or baked potatoes. Each potato is cut into very thin slices almost down to the bottom, so that it still holds together, and is then baked in the oven, sometimes sprinkled with cheese.

Serves 6–8 as a side dish

4 large baking potatoes (see tip), peeled and halved lengthways

15g (½oz) butter

4 tbsp vegetable oil

sea salt

1 Preheat the oven to 200°C/180°C fan/Gas 6.

2 Place the potatoes in a large saucepan of salted water and bring to the boil. Boil for 6–8 minutes or until parboiled – still firm in the middle. Drain and set aside until cool enough to handle.

3 Place the potatoes, cut side down, on a chopping board and, using a sharp knife, slice two-thirds of the way through each potato half at 5mm (¼in) intervals – this will create a fan effect when cooked.

4 Meanwhile, put the butter and oil into a large roasting tin and heat in the oven until piping hot. Add the potatoes, cut side down, to the hot oil and baste the tops. Roast in the oven for 45–60 minutes (depending on size), basting halfway through, until tender, crisp and golden. Serve at once, sprinkled with sea salt.

## MARY'S FOOLPROOF TIP

The best potatoes to use are varieties like Maris Piper or King Edward as they are firm and hold their shape.

# BUBBLE AND SQUEAK POTATO CAKES

Think fishcakes but made with cabbage and potato – delicious with fish, steak or bacon for brunch or just served with a fried egg on top. These are perfect for using up leftover mash; just make sure they are well seasoned and the cabbage is very finely shredded.

Makes 8 potato cakes

PREPARE AHEAD
Can be made up to 2 days ahead and reheated in a hot oven to serve. If cooking for a large number of people, fry in the morning, arrange on a baking sheet and reheat in a hot oven when needed.

FREEZE
The potato cakes freeze well uncooked – layer between greaseproof paper and wrap well.

---

1kg (2lb 3oz) King Edward potatoes, peeled and cut into even-sized cubes

25g (1oz) butter

350g (12oz) savoy cabbage, core removed and leaves finely shredded

50g (2oz) Parmesan cheese, grated

1 tbsp grainy mustard

50g (2oz) plain flour

a little sunflower oil, for frying

8 fried eggs, to serve (optional)

salt and freshly ground black pepper

1 Place the potatoes in a saucepan of salted water. Bring to the boil and cook for 20 minutes or until tender. Drain well (see tip), then add the butter, season with salt and pepper and mash together.

2 Cook the cabbage in boiling salted water for 5–6 minutes or until tender. Drain and refresh in cold water. Drain again and use your hands to squeeze out any excess water. Add the cooked cabbage and mashed potato to a large bowl.

3 Add the cheese and mustard to the bowl and mix well. Shape, using your hands, into eight even-sized cakes. Tip the flour on to a plate and dip each potato cake into the flour to coat both sides, tapping off any excess.

4 Heat the oil in a frying pan and fry the potato cakes over a high heat for 2–3 minutes on each side, until golden and piping hot. Serve each one topped with a fried egg, if you like, for a light supper.

---

## MARY'S FOOLPROOF TIP

Make sure the potatoes and cabbage are really well drained of excess water, as wet potato cakes will cause lots of spitting in the hot frying pan.

# GARLIC CRUSHED NEW POTATOES

**Pure comfort food and very moreish, this is a wonderful way of serving new potatoes. If they are very young and in season, you could leave the thin skins on. Don't forget to serve up the 'scratchings' from the roasting tin too: all the little nuggets of crunchy crushed potato and melted cheese – the best bits!**

Serves 4–6 as a side dish

PREPARE AHEAD
The potatoes can be boiled up to 8 hours ahead, ready to roast.

750g (1lb 10oz) new potatoes (unpeeled)

2 garlic cloves, crushed

50g (2oz), butter, melted, plus extra for greasing

30g (1oz) Parmesan cheese, coarsely grated

salt and freshly ground black pepper

1 Preheat the oven to 200°C/180°C fan/Gas 6 and grease a roasting tin with extra butter.

2 Put the potatoes (see tip) into a saucepan of salted water and bring to the boil. Boil for 15–18 minutes or until just tender, then drain and tip into the prepared roasting tin so they lie in a single layer (see tip).

3 Crush the potatoes (see tip), using a fork to squash them roughly. Mix the garlic with the melted butter and pour over the potatoes, tossing to coat. Season with salt and pepper and sprinkle with the Parmesan.

4 Roast in the oven for 30 minutes or until golden and crisp. Serve immediately.

## MARY'S FOOLPROOF TIPS

Cut any larger potatoes in half, so they are all similar in size before boiling; this ensures that they will cook in the same time.

The potatoes must lay in a single layer in the roasting tin, so that all the edges become crisp.

It is essential to crush the potatoes while they are still hot, so that they absorb the butter well.

# FOOLPROOF SALADS & VEGETABLES

Nowadays we eat an incredibly varied diet, which is largely due to the increasing influence of global cuisine on our day-to-day eating habits. As we travel more widely and eat out in restaurants more frequently, we're becoming more adventurous when it comes to the flavour and texture of our food. Add to this our ever-growing interest in healthy eating, and the demand for new and exciting salads and different ways of serving vegetables has never been greater.

SALADS

No longer relegated to the side dish, salads now come in many different forms, all packed with nutritious ingredients and bursting with flavour, making them a more than adequate main meal. Raw vegetables and salad leaves are best when they are in season and in their prime.

DO . . .

*Check for freshness* Salad leaves should be crisp and bright rather than pallid and limp.

*Keep salad leaves cool* Ideally store them in the salad drawer of your fridge. Keep lettuce whole rather than breaking off the leaves to store.

*Chop vegetables finely* When using raw vegetables in a slaw or salad, ensure you chop or shred them as finely as possible. Some food processors have handy attachments that can make this process quicker.

*Toss avocado in lemon juice* If preparing ahead, this will prevent avocado from going brown or discolouring.

*Check salad dressing for balance of flavour* A good salad dressing usually contains oil, vinegar or citrus juice, mustard and a touch of sweetness either from sugar or honey. The balance of flavour in a dressing is very much down to personal taste, but you can adjust this by experimenting with different ratios of oil and vinegar/citrus juice.

*Include nuts or seeds* to add texture, flavour and nutrients.

DON'T . . .

*Dress the salad too early* Salad leaves are best dressed just before serving, as the dressing can make the crisp salad leaves soggy over time.

VEGETABLES    Most vegetables can be enjoyed raw, either shredded finely in a salad, as crudités to serve with dips, or juiced along with fruit for a nutrient-packed drink. Raw vegetables do retain more nutrients than cooked vegetables, so it is good to include them in your diet in some form. Enjoy them in refreshing, crunchy and light salads during the warm summer months.

DO . . .

*Boil briefly for eating cold in salads* Vegetables such as broccoli, podded broad beans, peas and asparagus tips should be added to a pan of boiling water and boiled for the shortest time possible until the vegetables are just tender. Drain straight away. Overcooking will make the vegetables mushy and soft and impair their flavour and colour.

*Boil longer for eating warm* Add vegetables to boiling salted water (just enough water to cover the veg) and boil fast until they are completely tender.

DON'T . . .

*Discard the cooking water* If you are cooking vegetables for a roast and need water to make gravy, it's worth reserving any cooking water from the vegetables.

STEAMING    Vegetables can be cooked in the steam that is created from a pan of simmering water; as they don't come into direct contact with the water, this is a slower and gentler method of cooking that is often used for more delicate vegetables such as asparagus and pak choi. It is also thought to help prevent the loss of vitamins.

DO . . .

*Use a tight-fitting lid* to ensure the steam is kept within the steamer and cooks the vegetables efficiently.

DON'T . . .

*Overcrowd the pan* Ideally the vegetables should be in a single layer so that they cook evenly and at the same rate.

BRAISING    Vegetables are cooked in a covered pan with a small amount of water or stock and often a knob of butter too. This method is frequently used to cook more robust vegetables such as carrots, beetroot, cabbage and celery, and it helps to intensify the flavour of the vegetables.

DO . . .

*Keep an eye on the vegetables* As this method uses only a minimal amount of water, there is a chance that the pan will boil dry and the vegetables could burn. Using a tight-fitting lid will help prevent this, but it's best to check the vegetables occasionally.

DON'T . . .

*Braise green vegetables* In general, green vegetables don't react well to being braised; they tend to lose their colour and become mushy.

## STIR-FRYING AND SAUTÉING

These are the most effective ways of cooking tender vegetables such as mushrooms, onions and courgettes. Vegetables cooked this way are crisp and golden on the outside and tender in the middle. Other firmer vegetables can also be pan-fried, but they often need to be pre-cooked (blanched) before frying to ensure they become tender. Vegetables used in Asian-inspired stir-fry dishes are often very finely chopped to help speed up the cooking process.

DO . . .

*Use a large non-stick, wide-based frying pan or wok* This will allow you to use minimal fat, which will make it a healthier method of cooking.

*Preheat the pan* Ensure the pan is piping hot before use.

*Cut the vegetables into even-sized pieces* This will help them cook more evenly.

*Fry or sauté in batches* It's important not to overcrowd the pan, as this will create moisture and the vegetables will steam or stew rather than fry, which could make them soggy.

DON'T . . .

*Use butter on its own* If using butter, add a little oil too; this will help prevent the butter from burning.

## CHARGRILLING AND GRILLING

Many vegetables lend themselves to grilling or chargrilling – for example, peppers, aubergines, courgettes and onions. This allows the vegetables to be cooked quickly with minimal fat; it also gives them a lovely charred smokiness, which adds flavour.

DO . . .

*Use a minimal amount of oil* A small amount of fat is needed to prevent the vegetables from sticking, but too much may cause the grill to flare up. Rub the vegetables in a small amount of oil to lightly coat.

*Turn the vegetables* Whether you're using a grill or a griddle pan, the vegetables will need to be turned over to ensure they cook evenly.

DON'T . . .

*Set the grill to the highest setting* The temperature should be medium-high, otherwise the vegetables will burn on the outside and be raw in the middle.

**ROASTING**

This is one of the best ways to cook robust winter root vegetables such as parsnips, beetroot and potatoes, as well as squash and pumpkin. In the summer, Mediterranean-style roasted vegetables such as courgettes, peppers, aubergines, onions and garlic are also very popular. Roasting vegetables in a moderately hot oven allows their natural sugars to caramelise, which intensifies their flavour.

DO . . .

*Use a large roasting tin* – to ensure the vegetables roast rather than steam. The vegetables should be in a single layer, so divide them between two tins if need be.

*Cut the vegetables into equal-sized chunks* This will help them cook more evenly.

DON'T . . .

*Underestimate the quantity you need* Root vegetables shrink when cooked, so it can be tricky to predict how many you'll need. Always refer to a recipe to check the recommended weight per serving.

# POSH ROASTED VEGETABLES

**All the ingredients for ratatouille are here but presented in a particularly smart way. Delicious on its own as a vegetarian main, or serve with meat or fish as a side dish.**

Serves 6 as a side dish
or 4 as a main dish

PREPARE AHEAD
Can be made up to 8 hours ahead, and then reheated in the oven at 160°C/140°C fan/Gas 3 for 25 minutes.

2 medium
  aubergines, cut into
  1cm (½in) slices

2 red peppers,
  deseeded and cut into
  1cm (½in) slices

500g (1lb 2oz)
  courgettes, cut into
  1cm (½in) slices

6 tbsp olive oil

2 red onions,
  finely chopped

2 garlic cloves, crushed

500g (1lb 2oz)
  tomato passata

1 tsp caster sugar

1 small bunch of
  basil, chopped

50g (2oz) Gruyère
  cheese, grated

2–3 large tomatoes,
  each cut into
  8 wedges

2 tsp chopped
  thyme leaves

salt and freshly ground
  black pepper

1 You will need a 25cm (10in) shallow, round ovenproof dish (such as a ceramic quiche dish). Preheat the oven to 220°C/200°C fan/Gas 7 and line two large roasting tins with baking paper.

2 Place a mixture of aubergines, red peppers and courgettes in each roasting tin, spread in a single layer. Drizzle over 4 tablespoons of the olive oil and season well with salt and pepper. Roast in the oven for about 25 minutes until lightly browned and just soft (see tip). Set aside to cool and reduce the oven temperature to 200°C/180°C fan/Gas 6.

3 While the vegetables are roasting, heat the remaining oil in a large saucepan, add the onions and fry over a medium-high heat for 2–3 minutes. Add the garlic and fry for a further minute. Tip in the passata and season with the sugar and some salt and pepper. Bring to the boil, then cover with a lid, lower the heat and simmer for about 10 minutes or until the onions are soft and the sauce has reduced and thickened. Add the basil.

4 Spoon half the sauce into the base of the ovenproof dish and arrange half the roasted vegetables in a neat spiral pattern on top, then season with salt and pepper and sprinkle over the cheese. Spoon in and spread over the rest of the sauce, then arrange the remaining vegetables and the tomato wedges in a neat spiral pattern on top.

5 Sprinkle with the thyme, cover with foil and bake in the oven for 25 minutes or until bubbling. Cut into slices to serve.

## MARY'S FOOLPROOF TIP

Roasting the vegetables in advance drives off any excess liquid so the final dish isn't soggy.

# ROASTED CAULIFLOWER
# WITH LEMON PARSLEY DRESSING

I usually boil cauliflower, or cover it in a cheese sauce if I'm feeling a little more indulgent! Roasted cauliflower, however, is delicious and very healthy. It's best made and served straight away.

Serves 4 as a side dish

1 large cauliflower

2 tbsp olive oil

FOR THE DRESSING

4 tbsp olive oil

juice of 1 lemon

1 tbsp caster sugar

4 tbsp drained capers, roughly chopped

2 tbsp roughly chopped parsley

salt and freshly ground black pepper

1 Preheat the oven to 220°C/200°C fan/Gas 7.

2 Remove the outer leaves of the cauliflower and discard. Break the cauliflower into even-sized florets and place in a large, resealable freezer bag. Add 2 tablespoons of the oil and some salt and pepper and toss the florets in the bag so that they are coated in the seasoned oil.

3 Tip the coated florets into a shallow roasting tin and roast in the oven for 20–25 minutes until golden brown and crisp.

4 To make the dressing, mix together the oil, lemon juice, sugar, capers and parsley, and season with salt and pepper.

5 Tip the roasted cauliflower into a warmed serving dish, spoon over the caper dressing (see tip) and serve at once.

## MARY'S FOOLPROOF TIP

Pour the dressing over the hot cauliflower so it soaks in and adds flavour.

# ROSEMARY-ROASTED BEETROOT

**Beetroot is so good for you and is lovely served hot, roasted in the oven, rather than just added to a salad. While it's best served immediately, leftovers are delicious eaten cold, with a dollop of soft goat's cheese.**

Serves 4–6 as a
side dish

PREPARE AHEAD
Any leftovers can be cooled and stored, covered, in the fridge to eat later.

2 bunches of raw
  beetroot (about 8)

4 sprigs of rosemary,
  leaves finely chopped

1 tbsp olive oil

1 tbsp balsamic vinegar

1 tbsp light
  muscovado sugar

salt and freshly ground
  black pepper

1 Preheat the oven to 200°C/180°C fan/Gas 6.

2 Peel the beetroot (see tip) and cut into wedges, then put in a large, resealable freezer bag with the rosemary, oil, vinegar and sugar. Season well with salt and pepper and shake the bag to coat the beetroot wedges in the oil mixture.

3 Tip the coated beetroot into a roasting tin, spreading the wedges out in a single layer, and roast in the oven for 45–55 minutes, turning halfway through, or until just tender. Serve hot.

## MARY'S FOOLPROOF TIP

Use plastic gloves while preparing the beetroot to prevent staining your hands, and a plastic chopping board, as wooden ones stain easily.

# SPIRALIZED VEGETABLES

While I am not keen on too many new gadgets, a spiralizer is a great addition to the kitchen. With it you can make vegetable 'spaghetti' and serve as a delicious and healthy alternative to pasta and noodles. It's best to spiralize large, fat vegetables as thin ones will create strands that are too short. (See also tips.)

Serves 6 as a side dish

2 large fat carrots

2 large fat courgettes

2 tbsp olive oil

finely grated zest and juice of 1 lemon

1 tbsp finely chopped parsley

salt and freshly ground black pepper

1 Peel each carrot, place it in the spiralizer and follow the manufacturer's instructions to make long thin strands. Trim the top from each courgette (do not peel) and spiralize into strands.

2 Heat the oil in a large pan, add the carrot and courgette noodles and stir-fry over a high heat for 1–2 minutes. Season with salt and pepper, then add the lemon zest and juice and the chopped parsley. Toss together and serve in a heated dish.

## MARY'S FOOLPROOF TIPS

Use firm vegetables for this recipe and stir-fry really quickly – do not overcook.

Serve as you would standard noodles (such as for a stir-fry) or pasta (with a sauce) or as a vegetable on the side.

# CREAMED SPINACH

**This simple and delicious side dish is perfect for serving with fish or chicken.**

Serves 6 as a side dish

PREPARE AHEAD
The spinach can be wilted (see step 1) up to 6 hours ahead and kept, covered, in the fridge.

400g (14oz) baby spinach leaves

200ml (7fl oz) double pouring cream

40g (1½oz) Parmesan cheese, finely grated

1 small garlic clove, crushed

1 tbsp lemon juice

salt and freshly ground black pepper

1 Place the spinach in a colander and pour over a kettle of freshly boiled water to wilt the spinach. You may need to do this in batches. Douse the wilted spinach in cold water (see tip), then squeeze the leaves really well to remove as much water as possible.

2 Add the cream, Parmesan and garlic to a wide-based pan, stir together and bring to the boil. Boil for a minute to thicken slightly, then add the wilted spinach, season with salt and pepper and stir for a minute until piping hot.

3 Add the lemon juice and tip into a warmed serving dish to serve (see tip).

## MARY'S FOOLPROOF TIP

It's so important to douse the wilted spinach in cold water – this stops the cooking and keeps the bright green colour. If you omit this step, the spinach will turn a sludgy brown.

# RAINBOW COLESLAW

**Adding yoghurt to this coleslaw creates a slightly lighter version of the classic dish. It adds to the flavour, and chopped herbs make it taste very fresh too.**

Serves 6–8 as a
side dish

PREPARE AHEAD
The coleslaw can be made up to 6 hours ahead, adding the snipped chives to serve.

½ small white cabbage

½ small red cabbage

3 celery sticks

2 carrots, peeled

2 tbsp finely chopped
parsley

150g (5oz) natural
Greek yoghurt

8 tbsp full-fat
mayonnaise (see tip)

3 tbsp Dijon mustard
(see tip)

1½ tbsp caster sugar

1 tbsp white
wine vinegar

4 spring onions,
chopped

salt and freshly ground
black pepper

3 tbsp finely snipped
chives, to serve

1 Shred the cabbages, finely slice the celery and grate the carrots – either by hand or in a food processor, if you prefer, for speed and ease. Tip the prepared vegetables into a large bowl and add the chopped parsley.

2 In a separate bowl, mix together the yoghurt and mayonnaise with the mustard, sugar, vinegar and spring onions.

3 When you are ready to serve, pour the dressing over the prepared vegetables and toss well to combine. Season well with salt and pepper and sprinkle over the chives to serve.

## MARY'S FOOLPROOF TIPS

Using full-fat mayonnaise means the vegetables will remain coated in the dressing; low-fat mayonnaise can be used, but only if serving within a couple of hours.

You may like to increase the mustard if you want the coleslaw to be a little stronger.

# DESSERTS
# &
# PUDDINGS

# PASSION FRUIT POTS

**Divine, delicious, delectable – these creamy little pots are definitely worth devouring!**

Makes 6 pots

PREPARE AHEAD
Can be made up to a day ahead and kept in the fridge.

600ml (1 pint)
  double cream
100g (4oz)
  caster sugar
6 passion fruit
juice of 1 lime

1 Measure the cream into a saucepan, add the sugar and stir slowly over a low heat until the sugar has dissolved (see tip). Increase the heat and boil for about 3 minutes before removing from the heat.

2 Halve five of the passion fruit and scoop out the seeds, then add the seeds and juice to a food processor or blender and whizz until smooth – this will enhance the flavour. Pour through a sieve and add the juice to the warm cream and sugar mixture in the pan. Stir to combine – the cream will start to thicken – and discard the seeds left in the sieve.

3 Add the lime juice to the cream in the pan and stir – it will thicken further. Pour into six little glasses, such as shot glasses, and transfer to the fridge to set for a minimum of 3 hours or overnight.

4 To serve, cut the remaining passion fruit in half and divide the seeds and pulp between the glasses, spooning it on top of the set cream.

## MARY'S FOOLPROOF TIP

Make sure the sugar is dissolved completely in the cream otherwise the mixture will be grainy and not smooth once set.

# MANGO, LEMON AND LIME MOUSSE

**The ideal dessert to round off a dinner party – light, refreshing and very quick to prepare. Use best-quality lemon curd for the most intense flavour.**

Serves 4–6

PREPARE AHEAD
Can be made up to a day ahead and kept in the fridge.

2 ripe mangos
(about 400g/14oz
mango flesh)

300ml (10fl oz) double
pouring cream

finely grated zest and
juice of ½ lime

100g (4oz) luxury
lemon curd

1 Remove the skin from the mangos and slice the flesh away from the stone, cutting it into chunks. Reserve three large chunks and finely chop them before setting aside.

2 Put the remaining mango flesh into a food processor and whizz into a velvety purée.

3 Whip the cream in a bowl until beginning to form soft peaks (see tip). Fold the lime juice and lemon curd into the cream, swirling the mixture to give a ripple effect.

4 Take 4–6 small glasses or pots and spoon a little of the puréed mango into the bottom of each. Add a little of the lemon and lime cream mousse, then more of the mango, then the mousse, to give four layers in total (two each of the mango and mousse).

5 Decorate each glass or pot with the reserved chopped mango and the lime zest. Chill for an hour before serving.

## MARY'S FOOLPROOF TIP

Do not over-whip the cream – adding the lemon curd and lime juice will thicken it.

# LEMON AND ELDERFLOWER JELLIES

**Using homemade cordial for these jellies gives them a wonderful fresh flavour for a summery, light dessert, but if you only have shop-bought cordial, it will still be delicious.**

Makes 6 jellies

PREPARE AHEAD
Can be made up to 3 days ahead. Store in the fridge and decorate to serve.

8 leaves (20g) of
    gelatine (see tip
    on page 53)
250ml (9fl oz)
    elderflower cordial

FOR THE
LEMON SYRUP
75g (3oz) caster sugar
pared rind and juice
    of 2 lemons

TO SERVE
18 strawberries
2 tbsp icing sugar
150ml (5fl oz)
    whipping cream,
    whipped

1 To make the lemon syrup, measure the caster sugar and 100ml (3½fl oz) of water into a saucepan, then add the lemon rind and juice. Stir over a low heat until the sugar has dissolved and the liquid is clear. Bring to the boil, then remove from the heat and set aside to cool slightly, for 5 minutes, before removing the lemon rind.

2 Meanwhile, soak the leaves of gelatine in a bowl filled with cold water (see tip) and leave for 5 minutes until the leaves are soft. Squeeze out the liquid and add to the hot lemon syrup in the pan. Stir until dissolved and then pour in the elderflower cordial and 400ml (14fl oz) water, stirring to combine.

3 Pour the mixture into six wine glasses and leave to set in the fridge for a minimum of 4–6 hours.

4 To serve, pick out three small strawberries, with the green tops still attached, and cut each in half. Hull the remaining strawberries, slice into quarters and tip into a bowl. Add the icing sugar, stirring until it has dissolved and become syrupy. Divide the strawberries between the jellies, adding a spoonful to the top of each glass. Top with a dollop of whipped cream and half a small, green-tipped strawberry, before serving at room temperature.

## MARY'S FOOLPROOF TIP

Gelatine leaves are easy to use, but make sure you soak them in cold and not hot water, and squeeze them well after soaking.

# SUMMER PARTY GATEAU

Big, bold and beautiful, this gateau makes for a truly 'wow' moment when you carry it to the table. Add more fruits or even flowers for a very, very special occasion. You'll need to make the sponge mixture in two batches as it does not work whisking all eight eggs at once.

Serves 16

PREPARE AHEAD
The sponges are best made and filled a day ahead. This lets the cream set and hold the fruit.

FREEZE
The sponges can be frozen.

900ml (1½ pints) double cream

400g (14oz) raspberries

300g (11oz) blueberries

300g (11oz) blackberries

icing sugar, for dusting

FOR THE GENOESE SPONGES

8 eggs

250g (9oz) caster sugar

250g (9oz) self-raising flour

100g (4oz) butter, melted and cooled, plus extra for greasing

1 This recipe is best started the day before you want to serve it. You will need two 23cm (9in) round cake tins with 5cm (2in) sides. Preheat the oven to 180°C/160°C fan/Gas 4, then grease the tins with butter and line the bases with baking paper.

2 First make the sponges. Place four of the eggs and half the caster sugar in a bowl and, using an electric hand whisk or food mixer, whisk until thick, pale and fluffy. When you lift the whisk, the batter dropping from it should leave a trail in the mixture below (see tip overleaf).

3 Gently sift half the flour into the mixture, and carefully fold to combine (see tip overleaf). Drizzle half the cooled melted butter around the outside of the mixture and carefully fold in before pouring into one of the prepared cake tins.

4 Repeat steps 2 and 3 to make another sponge, and pour into the second tin.

5 Bake both sponges at the same time in the oven for about 30 minutes, or until pale golden, firm in the middle and shrinking away from the sides of the tin. If not baking on the same shelf, you may need to swap the tins around halfway through.

6 Remove from the oven and, after 10 minutes, release from the tins and set aside to cool completely on a wire rack. Remove the lining paper and, using a bread knife, slice each sponge in half horizontally to give four layers in total.

7 Whip the cream in a bowl until it forms firm peaks. Reserving 4 tablespoons for decorating the top of the cake, then divide the remaining whipped cream into three. Divide a mixture of the three different berries into three piles, reserving a handful of each for the top of the cake.

*Continues overleaf*

**8** Place one layer of sponge on a large plate, then spread with a third of the whipped cream, scatter over a third of the mixed berries (making sure they come around the edge of the cream, so they can be seen). Add another layer of sponge on top (see tip) and continue with cream and fruit until you have three layers, topped with a final layer of sponge.

**9** To decorate the top, spread the reserved cream in a small circle in the centre of the sponge and arrange the reserved mixed berries on top. Cover carefully with cling film and place in the fridge to settle – for a few hours, but overnight if possible. When you are ready to serve, dust the gateau with icing sugar and cut into slices.

### MARY'S FOOLPROOF TIPS

The stage where the mixture leaves a trail when the whisk is lifted is called the ribbon stage.

It is important to get a large volume of air into the mixture to create a light sponge. When folding in the flour and melted butter, be careful not to knock out any air from the mixture, and have your ingredients for the second sponge ready to go once you have made the first, so that the filled tin is not left standing for long.

Press down each sponge layer as it is topped so that the gateau holds together when cut.

# WHITE CHOCOLATE ICE CREAM

**This is a meringue-based ice cream, which gives you a smooth ice cream without needing to churn it in an ice-cream maker, making it much quicker and easier to prepare. It's best to buy a good-quality continental white chocolate for this recipe (see tip).**

Serves 6–8

FREEZE
Can be kept in the freezer for up to a month.

200g (7oz) good-quality white chocolate, broken into squares

4 eggs, separated

150g (5oz) caster sugar

300ml (10fl oz) double cream

1 tsp vanilla extract

1 Put the chocolate pieces into a heatproof bowl and melt over a pan of hot water. Stir until melted and smooth, taking great care not to let the chocolate get too hot. Set aside to cool just a little (but not too cold), but it should still be runny.

2 Meanwhile, make the meringue. Tip the egg whites into a large, spotlessly clean bowl and, using an electric hand whisk or food mixer, whisk on full speed until the whites form a stiff cloud. Gradually add the sugar, a teaspoon at a time, while still whisking on maximum speed, until all the sugar has been incorporated and the mixture is very stiff and glossy.

3 In a separate bowl, whip the double cream into soft peaks and fold in the vanilla extract. Beat the egg yolks with a fork and then fold into the whipped cream.

4 Take a large spoonful of the meringue and beat into the cream mixture to loosen it a little. Carefully fold the remaining meringue into the cream and then add the cooled melted chocolate, folding it in to combine. Gently mix until smooth, keeping the mixture light and airy.

5 Spoon into a freezerproof container, cover with a lid and leave in the freezer for a few hours, or overnight, until frozen. To serve, bring to room temperature for about 20 minutes to making scooping easier.

## MARY'S FOOLPROOF TIP

It's important to buy Belgian or other continental white chocolate as this has the highest cocoa butter content and is less likely to split or become lumpy when heated.

# BLACKBERRY RIPPLE

**A lovely dessert for autumn when blackberries fill the hedgerows, this is very easy to put together and great for making ahead.**

Serves 6

PREPARE AHEAD
Can be made up to a day ahead and kept chilled in the fridge.

450g (1lb) fresh
   blackberries
2 tbsp crème de cassis
75g (3oz) icing sugar
300ml (10fl oz)
   double cream
200g (7oz) natural
   Greek yoghurt

1 Tip 300g (11oz) of the blackberries into a bowl, add the cassis, toss together and set aside to marinate for 10 minutes.

2 Meanwhile, place the remaining blackberries in a food processor with the icing sugar and whizz together until smooth and runny. Pass the blackberry purée through a sieve into a bowl to remove the seeds.

3 Whip the cream in a separate bowl until it forms soft peaks (see tip), then fold in the yoghurt. Carefully fold in the blackberry purée to give a ripple effect (do not mix it in fully).

4 Reserving 12 of the marinated blackberries to decorate, divide the remaining fruit between six glasses. Spoon the blackberry ripple on top and decorate with the reserved blackberries. Chill in the fridge until needed.

## MARY'S FOOLPROOF TIP

Don't over-whip the cream or the ripple will have a grainy texture. The cream should be light so that the blackberry purée mixes in well.

# REAL HONEYCOMB ICE CREAM

**Dreamy, delicious and dangerous – take one mouthful and you'll want to devour the whole lot. Last Christmas, my grandchildren voted it their favourite ever ice cream! This also looks pretty made in ramekins (lined with cling film, like the loaf tin) and tipped on to individual plates to serve.**

Serves 8

PREPARE AHEAD
The extra honeycomb will keep for a week in an airtight container.

FREEZE
Can be kept in the freezer for up to a week.

4 tbsp golden syrup

150g (5oz) caster sugar

2 tsp bicarbonate of soda

600ml (1 pint) double cream

1 x 397g tin of full-fat condensed milk

1 You will need a 2lb (900g) loaf tin, lined with cling film (see tip on page 58). Lay a piece of baking paper (see tip) on your worktop, before making the honeycomb, with a baking sheet under it if your worktop isn't heatproof.

2 To make the honeycomb, measure the syrup and sugar into a medium-sized deep saucepan and stir gently over a low heat until the sugar has dissolved. Try not to let the mixture bubble until the sugar grains have disappeared. Once the sugar has completely dissolved, simmer for 5–6 minutes until you have a honey-coloured caramel. Watch it like a hawk – you want a light golden colour.

3 Immediately remove from the heat and tip in the bicarbonate of soda, beating with a wooden spoon until it is fully incorporated and the mixture is foaming. Pour on to the baking paper and scrape down the sides of the pan (taking care as the mixture is very hot). Leave for about 15 minutes until the honeycomb has hardened, then break into bite-sized pieces, reserving a third of these to decorate.

4 Whip the double cream to soft peaks, then stir in the condensed milk. Add the remaining two-thirds of the honeycomb to the cream mixture and stir to combine.

5 Pour into the prepared loaf tin, level the top and cover with cling film, then freeze for a minimum of 6 hours or overnight.

6 Tip out, remove the cling film and leave for 10 minutes before cutting into slices and serving immediately, sprinkled with the remaining honeycomb.

## MARY'S FOOLPROOF TIPS

It is vital to use non-stick baking paper for this – standard greaseproof paper will stick like glue to the honeycomb.

To clean your saucepan and wooden spoon, fill the pan with hot water and put the pan back on the heat, stirring occasionally. The set honeycomb will dissolve in the water and you won't have to scrub.

# FOOLPROOF DESSERTS & PUDDINGS

Desserts don't have to be difficult or require years of experience to be impressive and indulgent; in fact, some of the simplest puddings often turn out to be the biggest crowd pleasers. So if you're new to making desserts, don't be put off; there are plenty of recipes that are straightforward and go down extremely well.

When I'm entertaining at home I prefer to choose a dessert that can be prepared in advance, because it leaves one less thing to do when guests arrive, relieves stress and helps me feel properly prepared and in control. For this reason, chilled or frozen puds are often the best choice.

There are various skills to learn when making desserts, all of which you'll use time and time again in a wide variety of recipes. I've included a few key ones here.

## IN GENERAL

### DO . . .

*Use fresh eggs* These are easier to separate. Also, because they are sometimes used raw, it is important that they are super fresh and stored in a cool place beforehand.

*Take care when separating eggs* It's vital that no yolk comes into contact with the egg whites as this will affect their capacity to be whisked.

*Use a large clean bowl* It's crucial that the bowl used for whisking the egg whites is squeaky clean; any grease will interfere with the whisking process. Egg whites increase in volume when whisked, so it's best to use a large bowl.

*Use a large metal spoon or spatula* when folding the whisked egg whites into the base mixture, to retain as much air as possible to ensure the finished mousse is light.

### DON'T . . .

*Overheat chocolate* When melting chocolate for the base of recipes, allow it to melt slowly in a heatproof bowl set over a pan of hot water. As soon as it has fully melted, remove the bowl from the pan and set aside to allow the melted chocolate to cool slightly before combining with the egg yolks and sugar.

## USING GELATINE

Gelatine is used in a variety of chilled dessert recipes to give structure and help set them. It's used most often in classic fruit jellies or in combination with cream, such as panna cotta (see page 237) and some mousse and cheesecake recipes. There are a few things to keep in mind when using gelatine:

### DO . . .

*Pre-soak gelatine leaves* Leaf gelatine needs to be soaked in cold water for a few minutes before using to allow it to soften.

*Watch the temperature* The hot liquid base of your pudding should not be boiling when the gelatine is added or this will prevent the gelatine from setting properly.

*Guess quantities* Always use the specified type and quantity of gelatine in a recipe. Varieties (powdered and leaf form) and brands can vary in strength, so not following the guidelines in a recipe, or instructions on the packet, may cause your dessert to be too firm or prevent it from setting altogether.

## MAKING ICE CREAM

When making ice cream, it's wise to stick to the recipe; adding too much sugar, fruit or alcohol to the custard base can upset the balance and prevent it from freezing. In this book, I have given two ice cream recipes that are extremely simple and do not require whipping or using an ice-cream maker.

## MAKING CUSTARD

A classic egg custard (or crème anglaise) is an invaluable addition to your dessert repertoire. It can be poured over hot steamed puddings and crumbles or served chilled with summer berries, but it also forms the base for ice cream and baked and chilled custards such as crème brûlée and crème caramel (see pages 261 and 234). It is also a key ingredient in warm desserts like bread and butter pudding (see page 240).

Custard is made simply from egg yolks, sugar, cream and milk. Vanilla is usually added too, and other flavourings can be incorporated. I add a little cornflour to help thicken and stabilise the mixture too. Here are a few tips for making it.

DO . . .

*Combine well* Ensure the egg yolks, cornflour and caster sugar are well combined and smooth before adding the warm cream mixture.

*Use a heavy-based pan* The custard is less likely to catch on the bottom of the pan.

*Check the temperature* The warm cream mixture shouldn't be boiling when added to the egg yolks or this will cause the eggs to scramble. Bring the cream mixture almost to the boil, then remove from the heat and allow to cool slightly before combining with the egg yolk mixture.

*Stir constantly* Add the warm cream mixture gradually to the egg yolk mixture in a steady stream, stirring continuously to help them combine and prevent lumps.

*Strain the egg and milk mixture* This ensures that any small lumps are removed.

DON'T . . .

*Forget to clean the pan* When the creamy mixture has been added to the egg yolk mixture in the bowl, rinse the pan before returning the custard to it. This removes any milk residue, which could burn when reheated.

*Rush the process* When the custard is cooking in the pan, use only a very gentle heat and be patient. Stir the mixture constantly until it thickens; this should ensure a smooth, lump-free custard.

# PINEAPPLE, RASPBERRY AND MINT BOATS

**Sometimes it is nice to have a very simple fresh fruit dessert, especially after a more substantial main course. This is a different way of presenting fruit salad – as refreshing as it is spectacular. You could also do a variation of this recipe with wedges of ripe melon.**

Serves 4

PREPARE AHEAD
Can be assembled up to 8 hours ahead. Store in the fridge and dust with sugar just before serving.

1 small ripe pineapple (see tip)

175g (6oz) fresh raspberries

a small handful of mint sprigs

2 tbsp caster sugar (or to taste)

1 Slice the pineapple in half lengthways through the green stalk, leaving the leaves on for presentation. Slice in half again to give quarters.

2 Using a sharp knife, remove the core by standing each quarter upright and cutting downwards to slice away the triangle of tough core along the edge. Lay the pineapple down and slice carefully under the skin to remove the flesh from the skin in one piece.

3 Cut the flesh into thin slices, crossways, and sit back on the shell. Move each slice of pineapple in an alternate direction to give a slightly zigzag effect.

4 Dividing the raspberries between the pineapple wedges, arrange a few along the top of each 'boat', plus a few alongside, and sprinkle with mint sprigs. Serve chilled. Just before serving, dust with the caster sugar or to taste.

## MARY'S FOOLPROOF TIP

To check whether a pineapple is ripe, smell it. It should smell sweet and you should be able to pull one of the small leaves out easily.

# BAKED BOOZY NECTARINES

Quick to make and beautifully warming, this recipe works well with peaches too.
The marzipan caramelises and adds a delicious almond flavour, enhancing the natural
sweetness of the nectarines without being over-sweet, while the brandy and apple juice create
a light sauce. It is best made and served straight away.

Serves 4–6

6 nectarines (see tip)

4 tbsp brandy

2 tbsp apple juice
or water

150g (5oz) golden
marzipan, grated

1 Preheat the oven to 220°C/200°C fan/Gas 7.

2 Slice each nectarine in half and remove the stone, then place, cut side up, in an ovenproof dish that's wide enough to hold the nectarine halves in a single layer.

3 Mix the brandy with the apple juice or water and pour over the nectarines. Pile some grated marzipan into the centre of each nectarine half, filling the hole where the stone used to be.

4 Bake in the oven for about 15 minutes or until the marzipan is golden. Reduce the oven temperature to 180°C/160°C fan/Gas 4 and bake for a further 15 minutes until soft and tender. Serve warm with crème fraîche.

## MARY'S FOOLPROOF TIP

Try to buy nectarines that are just under-ripe. If they're ripe, cook them for slightly less time on the second baking.

# GINGER SEMIFREDDO WITH POACHED PEARS

**This must be the easiest 'cheat's' pudding ever – and it can be made ahead!
As it is semifreddo (half frozen), you need to remove it from the freezer in good time,
but it tastes good frozen too, so don't worry if you forget.**

---

Serves 6

PREPARE AHEAD
The semifreddo needs to be made at least
4 hours ahead; the pears can be poached
up to 8 hours ahead.

FREEZE
The semifreddo can be kept in the freezer
for up to a month.

---

300ml (10fl oz)
double cream

4 pieces of stem ginger,
finely chopped

8 tbsp ginger syrup
from the jar

300g (11oz)
Madeira cake

3 pears

150ml (5fl oz)
apple juice

1 You will need a 450g (1lb) loaf tin, lined with cling film (see tip on page 58).

2 Whip the cream in a bowl until beginning to form firm peaks. Fold in the chopped ginger and 2 tablespoons of the ginger syrup.

3 Slice the Madeira cake into layers horizontally (ideally three, but see tip) and place a third of the cake into the prepared loaf tin so that it sits neatly in the bottom of the tin. Spoon 2 tablespoons of the ginger syrup on to the cake and spread over half the ginger cream, levelling the top. Place the middle layer of cake on top, adding more ginger syrup and the rest of the ginger cream, and finish with a layer of cake with the remaining syrup spooned over. You will have three layers of cake and two of ginger cream.

4 Press down gently on top of the cake, then cover with cling film and freeze for at least 4 hours or overnight.

5 Remove the semifreddo from the freezer to soften for 30–40 minutes before serving. Meanwhile, poach the pears. Peel the pears and halve them, removing the cores. Lay the pear halves in a medium saucepan, cover with the apple juice and 50ml (2fl oz) water and bring to the boil. Cover with a lid, reduce the heat and simmer for about 15–20 minutes until just tender.

6 Cut the semifreddo into slices and the poached pears into thin slices, and serve.

---

## MARY'S FOOLPROOF TIP

Depending on the shape of your cake, you may need to cut the slices to fit your tin. Keep the pieces to a minimum for each layer – ideally one slice of cake per layer – as this will make it easier to cut when serving.

---

# CRÈME CARAMEL

**I've made a single large crème caramel here, but this recipe would be lovely in individual (150ml/5fl oz) ramekins too, cooked for 30–40 minutes. It is ideal for making ahead as the caramel becomes runny only once the custard has softened, which means leaving it in the fridge for at least 12 hours before serving.**

Serves 6

PREPARE AHEAD
Can be made up to 24 hours ahead and kept chilled in the fridge.

225g (8oz)
   caster sugar
a little butter,
   for greasing
4 eggs
2 egg yolks
1 tsp vanilla extract
600ml (1 pint)
   full-fat milk

1 You will need a 20cm (8in) round cake tin with 5cm (2in) sides and a fixed base. Preheat the oven to 140°C/120°C fan/Gas 1, then lay four sheets of baking paper in a roasting tin and sit the cake tin on top (see tip).

2 To make the caramel, measure 175g (6oz) of the sugar and 6 tablespoons of water into a stainless-steel pan (see tip) and heat over a low heat, stirring, until the sugar has dissolved and the liquid is clear. Once the sugar has dissolved, take your spoon from the pan, turn up the heat and boil – without stirring – until it turns a golden-brown caramel colour. Quickly pour the caramel into the cake tin so it forms a layer at the bottom. Once set, grease the sides of the cake tin with butter.

3 To make the custard, place the eggs and egg yolks in a bowl with the remaining sugar and the vanilla extract and whisk by hand to combine. Heat the milk in a pan until hot to the touch, then pour the hot milk into the bowl with the eggs and whisk rapidly until combined.

4 Pour the custard through a sieve into the caramel tin. Pour boiling water into the roasting tin until it comes halfway up the sides of the cake tin. Carefully slide the roasting tin into the oven and bake for 50–60 minutes until the custard is just set but with a slight wobble in the middle. Remove from the oven and leave the cake tin in the water for 30 minutes to cool down. Once cool (it will still have a slight wobble in the middle), transfer to the fridge to chill for about 12 hours.

5 Carefully run a knife around the edge of the crème caramel and then invert on to a dish (with shallow sides to catch the caramel sauce). Spoon into bowls to serve.

## MARY'S FOOLPROOF TIPS

The cake tin must not touch the roasting tin as this will conduct too much heat and overcook the custard. (This is why water is also added to the roasting tin.)

Caramel cannot be made in a non-stick saucepan as it will not change colour.

# LATTE PANNA COTTA WITH HAZELNUT BRITTLE

**With a delicate, creamy coffee flavour, this panna cotta – Italian for 'cooked cream' – is very elegant.**

Serves 8

PREPARE AHEAD

Can be made up to 2 days ahead if kept in the fridge. The brittle will last for 2 days in an airtight container out of the fridge (if moisture gets in, the caramel will soften).

sunflower oil,
  for greasing

2 tbsp instant
  coffee granules

2 tbsp boiling water

900ml (1½ pints)
  single cream

75g (3oz) caster sugar

7 leaves (13g) of
  gelatine (see tip on
  page 53)

FOR THE
HAZELNUT BRITTLE

150g (5oz)
  caster sugar

100g (4oz) whole
  shelled hazelnuts,
  lightly toasted (see tip)
  and finely chopped

1 You will need eight 150ml (5fl oz) timbale moulds or similar-sized ramekins. Line a baking sheet with baking paper and grease the moulds with sunflower oil.

2 First make the panna cotta. Measure the coffee granules into a mug, pour in the boiling water and stir until dissolved. Pour the cream into a saucepan, add the sugar and heat over a low heat, stirring gently, until the sugar has dissolved. Do not allow the mixture to boil. Pour in the coffee and stir before setting the cream mixture aside to cool for 5 minutes.

3 Place the gelatine leaves in a bowl of cold water and leave to soak for 5 minutes. Remove the leaves and squeeze well (see tip), then add to the warm coffee cream and stir until dissolved. Pour the mixture evenly into the moulds and transfer to the fridge to set. Chill for a minimum of 3 hours or until firm but with a slight wobble in the centre.

4 Next make the brittle. Measure the sugar and 100ml (3½fl oz) water into a stainless-steel saucepan (see tip on page 234) and stir over a medium heat until the sugar has dissolved. Remove the spoon from the pan and allow the mixture to boil over a high heat, without stirring, until the syrup is a pale caramel colour.

5 Add the toasted chopped hazelnuts and swirl the pan to coat the nuts in the caramel. Immediately pour on to the prepared baking sheet and leave to go cold and set hard. (Take care while it is still hot.) Once cold, chop into rough pieces.

6 To serve, dip each timbale mould in warm water to loosen the edges, invert on to a plate and scatter with the hazelnut brittle. Serve immediately.

## MARY'S FOOLPROOF TIPS

Be sure to squeeze out the gelatine leaves well, before adding to the warm cream.

To toast the hazelnuts, place on a baking tray and toast in the oven at 180°C/160°C fan/Gas 4 – or under the grill or in a dry frying pan on the hob – for 5 minutes, watching all the time and turning frequently so that they don't burn.

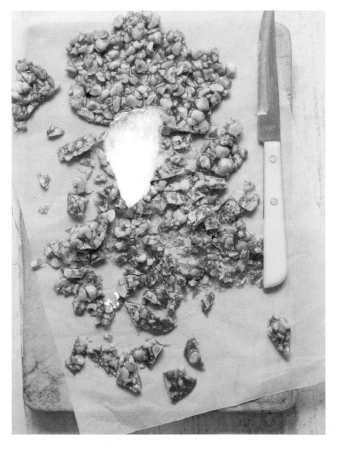

# BRIOCHE BREAD AND BUTTER PUDDING

**Made with brioche rather than a standard loaf, this is a lovely light pudding.
The lemon adds a fresh and delicate flavour to the otherwise creamy dish.**

Serves 6

1 x 300g (11oz)
  brioche loaf

50g (2oz) butter,
  melted, plus extra
  for greasing

100g (4oz) sultanas

3 tbsp demerara sugar

FOR THE CUSTARD

3 eggs

75g (3oz) caster sugar

150ml (5fl oz)
  double cream

600ml (1 pint)
  full-fat milk

1 tsp vanilla extract

finely grated zest of
  1 small lemon

1 You will need a 28cm (11in) wide-based round ovenproof dish, and a roasting tin large enough to place it in.

2 Cut the brioche loaf into 1.5cm (⅝in) slices and brush each slice with melted butter on both sides. Arrange the slices in a spiral in the buttered dish and scatter over the sultanas.

3 To make the custard, place all the ingredients in a large bowl and whisk together by hand until well mixed. Pour the custard over the brioche in the dish and gently press the exposed bread crusts down into the liquid. Sprinkle with the demerara sugar and leave to stand for about 30 minutes (see tip). While the pudding is standing, preheat the oven to 180°C/160°C fan/Gas 4 and grease the dish with a little butter.

4 Half-fill the roasting tin with boiling water, and place the ovenproof dish in this. Bake in the oven for about 40 minutes until golden on top and puffed up. The layers will shrink down a little on cooling. Serve warm with cream.

## MARY'S FOOLPROOF TIP

Allowing the dish to stand for 30 minutes once the custard has been poured over allows the brioche to soak up the custard and gives a light, fluffy pudding once cooked.

# RHUBARB EVE'S PUDDING

A delicious alternative to the traditional Eve's pudding, this uses rhubarb instead of apples. Try to find young rhubarb, if you can, to give a lovely pink colour. Best made and served on the day, it would be great for Sunday lunch.

Serves 6

400g (14oz) young pink rhubarb

finely grated zest and juice of 1 small orange

100g (4oz) demerara sugar

125g (4½oz) butter, softened

125g (4½oz) caster sugar

125g (4½oz) self-raising flour

1 tsp baking powder

2 eggs

1 You will need a 1.75-litre (3-pint) deep-sided ovenproof dish, about 20 x 25cm (8 x 10in) in size (see tip). Preheat the oven to 180°C/160°C fan/Gas 4.

2 Remove any outer leaves or dry parts of the rhubarb stems, then cut into bite-sized pieces and tip into the baking dish. Pour over the orange juice. Sprinkle over half the demerara sugar and mix to combine, making sure the rhubarb pieces are lying in an even layer.

3 To make the sponge, measure the butter into a bowl with the caster sugar, flour and baking powder, add the eggs and beat – either by hand with a wooden spoon or using an electric hand whisk – until combined. Stir in the orange zest, then spoon the batter over the rhubarb in the dish and sprinkle with the remaining demerara sugar.

4 Bake in the oven for 35–45 minutes or until the sponge is golden brown, well risen and springy to the touch. Serve warm with custard or cream.

## MARY'S FOOLPROOF TIP

The size of the dish matters for this recipe, because if it is too deep and narrow, the sponge will burn before the rhubarb is cooked. The fruit should lie in a single layer at the bottom.

# SWEET PIES
# &
# TARTS

# APPLE FRANGIPANE TART

With a base of crushed biscuits, rather than pastry, this tart is quick to make – no need for any rolling out or baking blind. The apple and almond go so well together too.

Serves 8–10

PREPARE AHEAD
Can be made a day ahead and reheated.

175g (6oz) digestive biscuits

75g (3oz) butter

200g (7oz) Bramley apples

FOR THE FRANGIPANE FILLING

75g (3oz) butter, softened

75g (3oz) caster sugar

2 eggs, beaten

75g (3oz) ground almonds

1 tsp almond extract

50g (2oz) flaked almonds

**1** You will need a 20cm (8in) round, loose-bottomed fluted tart tin with 3–4cm (1¼–1½in) sides. Preheat the oven to 200°C/180°C fan/Gas 6.

**2** Put the biscuits in a large, resealable freezer bag and bash with a rolling pin into fine crumbs. Melt the butter in a small pan, then add the biscuit crumbs and stir until coated in the butter. Tip into the tart tin and, using the back of a spoon, press over the base and up the sides of the tin to give an even layer. Chill in the fridge while you make the filling.

**3** Measure the butter and sugar into a food processor. Whizz for 2–3 minutes until creamy and fluffy. Add the eggs and whizz for another 10 seconds, then add the ground almonds and almond extract and blend for a further minute until combined.

**4** Peel the apples, remove the cores and cut into thin slices (see tip). Arrange the apple slices over the chilled biscuit base. Spoon the frangipane filling on top and spread out evenly, levelling the top and then sprinkling with the flaked almonds.

**5** Bake in the oven for 20–25 minutes until golden and set.

**6** Remove from the oven and leave to cool for 15 minutes. Remove from the tin (see tip) and transfer the tart, with the base of the tin still attached, on to a serving plate. Serve warm with cream, crème fraîche or ice cream.

## MARY'S FOOLPROOF TIPS

Peel the apples at the last minute to prevent them from going brown.

To remove a tart, cake or pie from a loose-bottomed tin, simply stand the tin on a can of beans, or a similar object, and push down the edges of the tin.

# APPLE AND APRICOT PIE

A traditional fruit pie that's full of flavour and lovely to tuck into when it's cold outside.
Serve warm with cream, custard or ice cream.

| Serves 6 | PREPARE AHEAD | FREEZE |
|---|---|---|
| | Can be made up to 8 hours ahead. | Freezes well. |

FOR THE PASTRY

225g (8oz) plain flour, plus extra for dusting

50g (2oz) caster sugar

100g (4oz) cold butter, cubed

1 egg, beaten, plus more beaten egg to glaze

FOR THE FILLING

250g (9oz) ready-to-eat dried apricots, each cut into 2–3 pieces

200ml (7fl oz) boiling water

1kg (2lb 3oz) Bramley apples, peeled, cored and thinly sliced

1½ tbsp cornflour

juice of ½ lemon

75g (3oz) caster sugar, plus extra for sprinkling

**1** You will need a 1.75-litre (3-pint) pie dish.

**2** Place the dried apricots in a bowl, pour over the boiling water, cover with cling film and leave to plump up for about 20 minutes. Drain when ready to use.

**3** To make the pastry, measure the flour into a food processor with the sugar and butter and whizz until the mixture looks like breadcrumbs. (Alternatively, place the dry ingredients in a bowl and rub in the butter with your fingertips.) Add the egg to the mixture with 1 tablespoon of cold water and mix again until a ball of dough is formed.

**4** Tip out on to a floured worktop and lightly knead until smooth. Wrap in cling film and chill in the fridge for about 15 minutes or until needed.

**5** Meanwhile, preheat the oven to 190°C/170°C fan/Gas 5. Place the drained apricots in a bowl and mix with the apple slices, cornflour, lemon juice and sugar. Tip this mixture into the pie dish.

**6** Place the chilled pastry on a floured worktop and roll out to about 3mm (⅛in) thick and 5cm (2in) wider than the top of your pie dish. Cut a 2cm (¾in) strip from around the edge of the pastry. Brush the lip of the pie dish with water and sit the strip of pastry on the top of it. Lay the pastry over the top of the filling and press into the strip of pastry around the lip.

**7** Trim off any excess, then crimp the edges and, using a sharp knife, make a hole in the centre of the pastry (see tip). Brush with beaten egg and then make some pastry leaves with the excess trimmings, and use to decorate the top of the pie.

**8** Sprinkle with caster sugar and bake in the oven for 40–50 minutes or until lightly golden on top and the pastry is cooked and the fruits are soft. Serve warm.

## MARY'S FOOLPROOF TIP

The hole in the pastry is necessary to let out the steam during baking and ensures the pie does not leak around the edges.

# FOOLPROOF PASTRY

Many people are fearful about making pastry, but they shouldn't be – it really is easy to make. The results are well worth the effort, too – see my Roasted Vegetable Quiche or Apricot and Apple Pie (pages 178 and 249). If you only learn to make one kind of pastry, shortcrust is the one to master. It's incredibly versatile and can be adapted to make savoury pies and quiches as well as sweet tarts and desserts.

**SHORTCRUST PASTRY**

Shortcrust pastry consists of three basic ingredients: plain flour, fat and a little liquid to bind it together. The general rule is a ratio of half fat to flour, though occasionally a higher proportion of fat is used to make a richer pastry.

Butter is most commonly used for shortcrust pastry, but a combination of lard or shortening and butter can be used to give a 'shorter' finish. Chilled water is usually added to bind the fat and flour together, and may be combined with egg yolk or whole egg to add richness. For sweet shortcrust pastry, a small amount of the flour is replaced with sugar to add sweetness and egg is added to enrich the pastry.

**MAKING SHORTCRUST PASTRY**

DO . . .

*Keep things cool* Make pastry somewhere cool, with cold hands if possible. Ensure your butter is chilled before using; this will prevent your pastry from becoming greasy.

*Rub the butter in quickly* You don't want the warmth from your hands to melt the butter.

*Add liquid carefully* Pour the water (and beaten egg or egg yolk, if using) very gradually into the 'breadcrumb' mixture. It is best to pour it in gradually, to avoid adding too much – you want to add only enough liquid to allow the pastry to come together. It's important that the pastry isn't too wet as this will make it sticky and difficult to work with.

*Speed it up* Use a food processor to combine the fat and flour if you like, but ensure you transfer it to a large bowl at the breadcrumb stage; it can be tricky to judge when to stop adding the liquid, creating a sticky dough.

DON'T . . .

*Overwork the dough* Once the dough has come together, don't be tempted to knead it for a long time, as this can make it tough. Simply shape into a smooth round and press into a disc, then wrap in cling film and chill in the fridge.

**RESTING AND ROLLING OUT**

DO . . .

*Let it rest* Don't be tempted to skip the resting step; it's important that the pastry is chilled and firms up before it is rolled out so that it will hold its shape when baked.

*Remove from the fridge before rolling out* Take the pastry out of the fridge a few minutes before rolling to make it easier to work with – although don't let it get warm.

*Select your tin in advance* Make sure you have the right size of tin or dish, and that it is prepared before you begin to roll out the pastry, so you can put it straight in.

*Give yourself space* Work on a large, clear and clean surface.

DON'T . . .

*Use too much flour for rolling* Only use a light dusting of flour when rolling out pastry, otherwise you risk upsetting the balance of ingredients in the dough and making it too dry. You can also roll out pastry between sheets of baking paper or cling film if you prefer not to use flour.

## LINING YOUR TIN AND BAKING BLIND

DO . . .

*Prick the base several times with a fork* This helps the pastry to cook evenly.

*Line your pastry case* with foil or baking paper before filling with baking beans.

*Chill before baking blind* This helps to prevent it from shrinking as it cooks.

*Seal it with egg white if your filling is wet* After the initial 15 minutes of blind baking, remove the baking beans and brush the base of the pastry case with a little beaten egg white. Bake for a further 5 minutes. This helps it to crisp up and create a seal before a wet filling is added.

*Trim excess pastry while warm* for a smooth finish.

DON'T . . .

*Roll your pastry out too small* Roll the pastry out a little larger than your tin so that it overhangs the sides. This allows for shrinkage in the oven.

*Press with your fingers* Use a floured nugget of the pastry trimmings to press the pastry into the sides of the tin so that it fits well and so that you don't accidentally damage the pastry case with your fingers.

## PREPARE AHEAD

You can make pastry up to 2 days ahead and store it, wrapped in cling film, in the fridge. Just make sure you remove it from the fridge a few minutes before rolling out to allow it to become soft enough to roll. You can freeze unbaked and baked pastry cases in their tins – unbaked cases up to 3 months and baked cases for up to 4 months.

## OTHER TYPES OF PASTRY

It's rarely necessary to make your own filo or puff pastry as the ready-made versions are of a high standard and ideal for everyday cooking.

*Puff pastry* needs to be kept very cool due to its high fat content, so always chill it before baking.

*Filo pastry* can dry out very quickly, so keep the rest of the sheets covered with a damp tea towel while you are working with it.

# SPICED APPLE AND MINCEMEAT STRUDEL

**This scrumptious strudel, with its mincemeat and apple filling, would be great to serve at Christmas, as well as helping to use up any windfalls from the garden.**

Serves 6

PREPARE AHEAD
Can be made up to a day ahead and stored in an airtight container.

FREEZE
Freezes well uncooked.

6 sheets (each 25 x 45cm/10 x 18in) of filo pastry

60g (2½oz) butter, melted

25g (1oz) fresh white breadcrumbs

FOR THE FILLING

450g (1lb) cooking apples, peeled, cored and cut into 2cm (¾in) dice

200g (7oz) good mincemeat from a jar

50g (2oz) demerara sugar

1 tsp mixed spice powder

1 tsp ground cinnamon

FOR THE ICING

175g (6oz) icing sugar, sifted

juice of 1 lemon

25g (1oz) flaked almonds, toasted (see tip on page 237)

**1** Preheat the oven to 200°C/180°C fan/Gas 6.

**2** First prepare the filling. Put the apples into a large bowl with the mincemeat, demerara sugar and spices and mix together to combine.

**3** Place two sheets of filo pastry side by side (long edges together) on a piece of baking paper – they should overlap slightly (by about 5cm/2in) where they meet in the middle – to form a 45cm (18in) square. Brush with melted butter, then place two more sheets of filo pastry on top, at right angles to the first layer and slightly overlapping where they join. Brush again with melted butter. Repeat with the final two sheets of pastry, laying them in the same direction as the first two sheets, forming a 45cm (18in) square (see tip on page 66).

**4** Sprinkle the breadcrumbs over the pastry (see tip), then spoon the filling along one-third of the filo square in a long log shape, leaving a gap of at least 5cm (2in) from the edge of the pastry. Fold the sides in over the filling and brush with butter, then roll up the strudel to make a large sausage shape about 30cm (12in) long. Use the baking paper to help to roll it up firmly. Make sure the ends of the pastry are sealed and brush the top with more melted butter before transferring the strudel with the paper to a baking sheet.

**5** Bake in the oven for about 35 minutes until the pastry is golden and crisp all over.

**6** For the icing, mix the icing sugar with the lemon juice in a bowl to make a fairly thick icing. Drizzle over the strudel and then sprinkle with toasted almonds. Transfer to a serving plate and serve warm with cream.

## MARY'S FOOLPROOF TIP

The breadcrumbs soak up any juices from the apples as they cook, helping prevent the pastry from becoming soggy.

# BANANA AND HONEY GALETTES

These delicious pastries are best eaten straight away and served warm. Children will love them, especially with a dollop of vanilla or butterscotch ice cream on the side.

Makes 6 galettes

3 ripe bananas

2 tbsp runny honey

½ x 375g packet of ready-rolled, all-butter puff pastry

plain flour, for dusting

5 tbsp full-fat mascarpone cheese

1 small egg beaten with 1 tbsp milk

2 tbsp demerara sugar

**1** Preheat the oven to 200°C/180°C fan/Gas 6 and put a baking sheet in the oven to get very hot.

**2** Peel the bananas and cut into 5mm (¼in) discs. Tip into a bowl, drizzle over the honey and toss together so the banana slices are coated.

**3** Roll the pastry out on a work surface lightly dusted with flour into a rectangle measuring 20 x 28cm (8 x 11in). Cut the pastry in half lengthways and in three across to give six squares.

**4** With a sharp knife, make a cut 1cm (½in) in from the edge of each square to create a border. Prick the inner square of each galette a few times with a fork.

**5** Dividing the mascarpone between the six galettes, spread it over the inner square of each galette. Top with neat rows of honey-coated banana slices. Brush the pastry borders with egg wash and then sprinkle the demerara sugar over both the bananas and the pastry.

**6** Remove the heated baking sheet from the oven. Arrange the galettes on the baking sheet (see tip) and return to the hot oven to bake for 20–25 minutes or until the bananas are beginning to caramelise and the pastry is golden and cooked through. Enjoy with cream, or a scoop of vanilla ice cream.

## MARY'S FOOLPROOF TIP

Putting the galettes on a hot baking sheet ensures the pastry is crisp underneath and there are no soggy bottoms!

# MINI CHOCOLATE TARTS

**These indulgent little tarts look so impressive: great for serving at the end of a meal as part of a dessert – perhaps served with the lemon tarts on page 260 – or to go with coffee.**

| Makes 24 tarts | PREPARE AHEAD | FREEZE |
|---|---|---|
| | Can be made up to a day ahead. | The cooked tart cases freeze well raw or after baking blind. |

**FOR THE CHOCOLATE PASTRY**

80g (3oz) plain flour, plus extra for dusting

15g (½oz) cocoa powder

50g (2oz) cold butter, cubed

2 tbsp icing sugar, plus extra for dusting

1 egg yolk, beaten

**FOR THE FILLING**

50g (2oz) butter

75g (3oz) dark chocolate (no more than 40–50% cocoa solids), broken into squares

40g (1½oz) plain flour

75g (3oz) caster sugar

2 eggs, beaten

**1** You will need an 8cm (3in) fluted pastry cutter, a 24-hole mini muffin tin and some baking beans.

**2** First make the pastry. Measure the flour and cocoa powder into a food processor with the butter and icing sugar and whizz until the mixture looks like breadcrumbs. (Alternatively, place the dry ingredients in a mixing bowl and rub in the butter with your fingertips.) Add the egg yolk and 1 tablespoon of cold water and mix again until a ball of dough is formed.

**3** Transfer the dough to a lightly floured work surface and roll out very thinly to 1–2mm (¹⁄₁₆in) thick. Cut out 24 discs with the pastry cutter and use these to line the moulds of the muffin tin, pressing each disc into the sides of the mould. Prick the base of each disc with a fork and place in the freezer for 30 minutes to firm up.

**4** Meanwhile, preheat the oven to 200°C/180°C fan/Gas 6.

**5** Line the chilled pastry cases with squares of baking paper and fill with baking beans. Bake in the oven for 8–10 minutes or until the pastry is cooked. Remove the beans and paper and return to the oven for 3–4 minutes to dry out completely.

**6** Meanwhile, make the filling. Melt the butter in a saucepan, add the chocolate and stir over a low heat until melted (see tip). Remove from the heat, tip in the flour and caster sugar and whisk by hand to combine, then add the eggs and whisk again. Pour into a jug then divide evenly between the pastry cases.

**7** Bake for about 8 minutes or until just set and a light crust has formed on top. Remove from the tin and allow to cool before serving warm or cold.

## MARY'S FOOLPROOF TIP

Do not overheat the chocolate mixture or it may split.

# MINI LEMON TARTS

These are similar to the chocolate tarts on page 258. They are divine served together – a lovely contrast in colours and flavours. (Pictured on previous page.)

Makes 24 tarts

PREPARE AHEAD
Can be made up to a day ahead.

FREEZE
The cooked tart cases freeze well raw or after baking blind.

FOR THE PASTRY

100g (4oz) plain flour, plus extra for dusting

50g (2oz) cold butter, cubed

2 tbsp icing sugar

1 egg yolk, beaten

FOR THE FILLING

2 medium eggs, beaten

finely grated zest of 1½ lemons and 75ml (3fl oz) lemon juice

75ml (3fl oz) double cream

100g (4oz) caster sugar

**1** You will need an 8cm (3in) fluted pastry cutter, a 24-hole mini muffin tin and some baking beans

**2** First make the pastry. Measure the flour into a food processor with the butter and icing sugar and whizz until the mixture looks like breadcrumbs. (Alternatively, place the dry ingredients in a mixing bowl and rub in the butter with your fingertips.) Add the egg yolk and 1 tablespoon of cold water and mix again until a ball of dough is formed.

**3** Transfer the dough to a lightly floured work surface and roll out very thinly to 1–2mm (1⁄16in) thick. Cut out 24 discs with the pastry cutter and use these to line the moulds of the muffin tin, pressing each disc into the sides of the mould. Prick the base of each disc with a fork and place in the freezer for 30 minutes to firm up.

**4** Meanwhile, preheat the oven to 200°C/180°C fan/Gas 6.

**5** Line the chilled pastry cases with squares of baking paper and fill with baking beans. Bake in the oven for 8–10 minutes or until the pastry is cooked. Remove the beans and paper and return to the oven for 3–4 minutes to dry out completely.

**6** Whisk the filling ingredients together in a jug and then pour into the pastry cases, dividing the mixture evenly between them. Bake for about 10 minutes or until just set, but still with a slight wobble in the middle of each tart (see tip). Carefully remove from the tin and leave to cool before serving warm or cold.

## MARY'S FOOLPROOF TIP

Check on the tarts while in the oven so that they do not overbake – this could make the custard curdle.

# CRÈME BRÛLÉE TART

Crème brûlée in a pastry case – what could be more wicked! For a crunchy caramel topping, it's best eaten within a few hours. The caramel will become runny if you keep it until the following day – though it will still be delicious! (Pictured overleaf.)

Serves 8

**PREPARE AHEAD**
The custard tart can be made up to a day ahead. Pour over the caramel up to 6 hours ahead.

**FREEZE**
The pastry can be made ahead of time and frozen.

4 eggs, beaten
250g (9oz) caster sugar
600ml (1 pint) double pouring cream
2 tsp vanilla extract

FOR THE PASTRY

175g (6oz) plain flour, plus extra for dusting
100g (4oz) butter, cubed, plus extra for greasing
25g (1oz) icing sugar
1 egg, beaten

**1** You will need a 23cm (9in) round, deep, loose-bottomed fluted tart tin and some baking beans.

**2** First make the pastry. Measure the flour and butter into a food processor and whizz until the mixture looks like breadcrumbs (or place in a mixing bowl and rub the butter into the flour with your fingertips). Add the icing sugar and egg and mix again to form a smooth dough.

**3** Roll out the dough on a work surface lightly dusted with flour, into a circle large enough to line the tart tin and about 3mm (⅛in) thick, leaving a generous edge to allow for shrinking in the oven (see tip overleaf). Prick the base and sides of the pastry in the tin and chill in the fridge for 15 minutes. While the pastry is chilling, preheat the oven to 190°C/170°C fan/Gas 5 and grease the tin with butter.

**4** Line the pastry case with baking paper, fill with baking beans and bake blind for about 15 minutes. Remove the paper and the beans, then return to the oven and bake for a further 5 minutes. Take out of the oven and set aside, then reduce the oven temperature to 160°C/140°C fan/Gas 3.

**5** To make the custard, add the eggs and 100g (4oz) of the caster sugar to a bowl and whisk together by hand. Add the cream and vanilla extract and whisk until smooth. Strain the mixture through a sieve set over a jug and then pour into the pastry case.

*Continues overleaf*

# CRÈME BRÛLÉE TART *Continued*

**6** Bake for 50–60 minutes until the custard is set around the edges but still has a wobble in the centre – make sure it does not brown (see tip). Remove from the oven, then set aside to cool down completely before chilling in the fridge until set and cold.

**7** To make the caramel, place the remaining 150g (5oz) of sugar in a stainless-steel saucepan (see tip on page 234), add 4 tablespoons of water and set over a low heat, stirring gently, until the sugar has dissolved. Take your spoon out of the pan, turn up the heat and boil – without stirring – until the syrup turns a caramel colour. Remove from the heat and immediately pour the caramel over the cold tart (keeping the caramel within the pastry edges), then carefully tip the tart to ensure all the custard is covered. Leave to set at room temperature for about an hour.

**8** To serve, trim the overhanging pastry edges from around the edge of the tart. Bash the caramel (it will be rock hard) with the back of a spoon and cut the tart into wedges.

## MARY'S FOOLPROOF TIPS

Leave the edges of pastry overhanging the tin when baking blind – they can be trimmed off later, once the tart has been cooked. This will ensure no shrinkage at the edges, and a good lip to hold in the custard, and then the caramel topping.

Do not overcook the custard or bubbles will appear. If the custard starts to brown, and is cooking too quickly, turn the oven temperature down a little, and keep an eye on the tart.

# APPLE AND BLACKBERRY COBBLER

This pudding is great for using home-grown apples and foraged blackberries – the soft, scone-like topping is offset by the sharpness of the fruit. Blackcurrants would work well too in place of the blackberries.

Serves 6

1kg (2lb 3oz) cooking apples, peeled, cored and cut into 2cm (¾in) dice

200g (7oz) blackberries

100g (4oz) demerara sugar

icing sugar, for dusting

FOR THE COBBLER

150g (5oz) self-raising flour

50g (2oz) cold butter, cubed, plus extra for greasing

50g (2oz) caster sugar

1 egg, beaten

4 tbsp milk

1 You will need a 20cm (8in) round ovenproof dish. Preheat the oven to 200°C/180°C fan/Gas 6 and grease the dish with butter.

2 Place the apples, blackberries and demerara sugar in the prepared dish and mix together.

3 To make the cobbler, measure the flour and butter into a food processor and whizz until the mixture is like breadcrumbs (or place in a mixing bowl and rub the butter into the flour with your fingertips). Add the caster sugar, egg and milk and mix again until combined. It should be like a wet scone mix.

4 Spoon blobs of the cobbler mixture over the fruit in the dish (see tip), then bake in the oven for 30–35 minutes or until golden brown on top and the fruit is soft and bubbling.

5 Dust with icing sugar and serve warm with cream.

## MARY'S FOOLPROOF TIP

Spooning the batter over the fruit in blobs gives the desired effect when baked. Don't worry if there are a few gaps – the mixture will blend together a bit more once it's cooked.

# CAKES & BISCUITS

# GLUTEN-FREE APPLE AND COCONUT CAKE

**Made without flour, this cake is perfect for anyone with a gluten intolerance,
and ideal for using up any apples left for too long in the fruit bowl.**

Serves 8–10

PREPARE AHEAD
The cake can be made and iced up to a day ahead. Store in an airtight container.

2 eating apples,
  peeled, cored and
  finely diced (see tip)
finely grated zest of
  1 lemon and juice
  of ½ lemon
225g (8oz)
  caster sugar
225g (8oz) butter,
  softened, plus extra
  for greasing
200g (7oz)
  ground almonds
6 eggs, beaten
½ tsp vanilla extract
1 tsp gluten-free
  baking powder
3 tbsp desiccated
  coconut

FOR THE
COCONUT ICING
100g (4oz)
  butter, softened
200g (7oz) icing
  sugar, sifted
3 tbsp full-fat coconut
  milk (see tip)

1 You will need a 23cm (9in) round, loose-bottomed cake tin with deep sides. Preheat the oven to 180°C/160°C fan/Gas 4, then grease the tin with butter and line the base with baking paper.

2 Put the diced apples in a saucepan, add the lemon zest and juice and cook, stirring regularly, over a medium heat for 4–5 minutes. Cover with a lid, reduce the heat and simmer for about 15 minutes or until soft. Set aside to cool.

3 Measure the caster sugar and butter into a bowl with the almonds, eggs, vanilla extract and baking powder, and beat together with an electric hand whisk to combine.

4 Carefully fold in the cold apple mixture and 2 tablespoons of the desiccated coconut. Spoon into the prepared tin, levelling the top, and bake in the oven for about 45 minutes or until golden and springy to the touch.

5 Take out of the oven and set aside to cool down completely before removing from the tin (see tip on page 246).

6 To make the icing, measure the butter and icing sugar into a bowl. Mix to combine, gradually adding the coconut milk a tablespoon at a time and mixing in carefully (see tip).

7 Spread the icing over the top of the cold cake and sprinkle with the remaining coconut. Cut into wedges to serve.

## MARY'S FOOLPROOF TIPS

Keep the apple pieces small otherwise, once incorporated into the cake batter, they may sink to the bottom of the cake during baking.

Coconut milk can be thick or thin, depending on the brand; choose one that's the consistency of single cream.

If the icing looks as if it has separated (perhaps if the coconut milk was added too quickly), add another tablespoon of icing sugar (sifted) to make it smooth again.

# CARROT AND BANANA CAKE

**This combination may sound a little strange, but I have always put banana in my carrot cake to give a moist sponge. The banana also makes the texture slightly more dense rather than light and springy.**

Serves 8–12

PREPARE AHEAD
The cake can be made and iced up to a day ahead.

FREEZE
The sponges freeze well without the icing.

## FOR THE CAKE

4 eggs, beaten

275g (10oz) caster sugar

250ml (9fl oz) sunflower oil, plus extra for greasing

275g (10oz) self-raising flour

2 tsp baking powder

2 small ripe bananas, peeled and mashed (about 200g/7oz)

2 medium carrots (150g/5oz), peeled and coarsely grated (see tip)

## FOR THE ICING

280g (10oz) full-fat cream cheese

150g (5oz) butter, softened

1 tsp vanilla extract

250g (9oz) icing sugar, sifted

**1** You will need two 20cm (8in) round sandwich tins. Preheat the oven to 180°C/160°C fan/Gas 4, then grease the tins with sunflower oil and line the bases with baking paper.

**2** Make the cake. Place the eggs, caster sugar and sunflower oil in a bowl and beat until just combined. Measure the remaining cake ingredients into the same bowl and beat together well. Divide the mixture evenly between the tins and smooth the tops.

**3** Bake in the oven for 35–40 minutes until golden, firm in the middle and shrinking away from the sides of the tins. Set aside to cool for 10 minutes, then remove from the tins and leave to cool on a wire rack.

**4** Meanwhile, make the icing. Whisk the cream cheese and butter together in a bowl, either by hand or using an electric hand whisk. Add the vanilla extract and icing sugar and whisk again until smooth.

**5** Once the sponges are cold, use half the icing to sandwich them together. Sit on a plate and use the remaining icing to cover the top of the cake in a pretty swirl (see tip). Place in the fridge to chill for at least an hour and then cut into wedges to serve.

## MARY'S FOOLPROOF TIPS

Coarsely grate the carrots; if they are finely grated, too much water comes out of them during cooking and results in a wet cake.

The icing is fairly soft but will firm up once chilled.

# FRUITCAKE LOAVES

I prefer making two 450g (1lb) loaf cakes, rather than one large cake cooked in a 900g (2lb) loaf tin, as the smaller cakes are less likely to dry out around the edges. These are perfect for preparing ahead as you can eat one and freeze one for another day.

| Makes 2 loaves and each serves 8 | PREPARE AHEAD<br>Can be made up to 2 days ahead and stored in an airtight container. | FREEZE<br>The cooked cakes freeze well. |
| --- | --- | --- |

150g (5oz) caster sugar

150g (5oz) butter, softened, plus extra for greasing

200g (7oz) self-raising flour

200g (7oz) glacé cherries, washed and chopped (see tip)

200g (7oz) sultanas

2 eggs

1 tbsp milk

finely grated zest of 2 lemons

25g (1oz) flaked almonds

1 You will need two 450g (1lb) loaf tins. Preheat the oven to 160°C/140°C fan/ Gas 3, then grease the tins with butter and line with baking paper.

2 Measure all the ingredients (see tip) except the flaked almonds into a bowl and mix together until combined. Divide evenly between the two prepared tins and level the tops. Sprinkle with the almonds.

3 Bake in the oven for about 1¼ hours or until golden on top and firm to the touch. Set aside to cool for about 10 minutes before turning out on to a wire rack to cool down completely. Cut into slices to serve.

## MARY'S FOOLPROOF TIPS

Wash the syrup from the cherries, leave to drain in a sieve and then dry thoroughly on kitchen paper – this prevents them from sinking to the bottom of the cakes during baking. If the cherries are still sticky when you chop them, it is worth rinsing and drying them again.

Measure the ingredients carefully – the cake batter is meant to be quite firm. If it is too loose, all the fruit could sink to the bottom of the cakes.

# HOLIDAY BANANA CAKE

**When we were on holiday last year, some friends came over to our villa for a barbecue and brought this delicious cake with them, still warm from the oven. It's a great way to use overripe bananas as they give the best flavour.**

Serves 8–10

PREPARE AHEAD
Can be made a day ahead.

FREEZE
Freezes well.

125ml (4fl oz) sunflower oil, plus extra for greasing

200g (7oz) caster sugar

1 tsp vanilla extract

175g (6oz) plain flour

1 tsp bicarbonate of soda

½ tsp ground cinnamon

2 eggs, beaten

3 small ripe bananas, peeled and mashed (about 300g/11oz)

1 You will need a 900g (2lb) loaf tin. Preheat the oven to 180°C/160°C fan/Gas 4, then grease the tin with oil and line the base with a strip of baking paper.

2 Place all the ingredients in a large bowl and, either by hand or using an electric hand whisk, beat together for 1 minute. Spoon into the prepared tin and level the top.

3 Bake in the oven for about an hour until lightly golden on top, springy to the touch and coming away from the sides of the tin (see tip).

4 Cool in the tin for 10 minutes, then remove and leave to cool on a wire rack. Cut into slices and serve plain or spread with butter.

## MARY'S FOOLPROOF TIP

To make sure the centre of the cake is cooked, test by inserting a fine metal skewer – if it comes out clean, the cake is ready.

# CARDAMOM SPONGE
# WITH WHITE CHOCOLATE ICING

Cardamom gives a delicate flavour to this moist sponge, combining surprisingly well with the white chocolate icing. When you are grinding the cardamom, be sure to crush the seeds only, not the pods, as these won't soften enough during baking to become absorbed into the cake, and can lead to a gritty texture. The shards of white chocolate are a simple but impressive decoration, and make this a wonderful cake for a special occasion.

Serves 8

**PREPARE AHEAD**
The cake can be made and iced up to a day ahead.

**FREEZE**
Freezes well without the icing.

225g (8oz) butter, softened, plus extra for greasing

4 eggs, beaten

225g (8oz) caster sugar

225g (8oz) self-raising flour

1 tsp baking powder

12 cardamom pods

50g (2oz) good-quality white chocolate, to decorate

FOR THE ICING

100g (4oz) good-quality white chocolate (see tip on page 221)

50g (2oz) butter, softened (see tip overleaf)

75g (3oz) full-fat cream cheese

200g (7oz) icing sugar, sifted

½ tsp vanilla extract

**1** You will need two 20cm (8in) round sandwich cake tins. Preheat the oven to 180°C/160°C fan/Gas 4, then grease the tins with butter and line the bases with baking paper.

**2** Place the butter and eggs in a large mixing bowl with the sugar, flour and baking powder and beat together, by hand or using an electric hand whisk, until combined.

**3** Bash the cardamom pods with a rolling pin on a chopping board to release the seeds. Grind the seeds until fine using a pestle and mortar then stir this into the cake batter. Pour the batter into the prepared tins and smooth the tops.

**4** Bake in the oven for about 25 minutes until golden brown and springy to the touch. Allow to cool in the tins for 5 minutes and then turn out and leave to cool on a wire rack.

**5** Make the icing. Place the white chocolate in a heatproof bowl set over a pan of gently simmering water. Stir until melted and smooth, taking great care not to let the chocolate get too hot (see tip overleaf). Set aside to cool and thicken a little.

*Continues overleaf*

# CARDAMOM SPONGE WITH
# WHITE CHOCOLATE ICING *Continued*

**6** Whisk the butter and cream cheese together until fluffy and soft. Whisk in half the icing sugar, then add the vanilla extract and remaining icing sugar and whisk again. Stir in the melted white chocolate to combine and then transfer to the fridge to chill for about 20 minutes until thickened enough to spread on the cake (see tip).

**7** Divide the icing between the two cakes, spreading half on one, sandwiching with the second cake and using the rest of the icing to cover the top. Use a sharp knife to cut or shave the remaining white chocolate into angular shards and then arrange these over the top of the cake to make an impressive decoration. Cut into wedges to serve.

······················································································

## MARY'S FOOLPROOF TIPS

Make sure the butter for the icing is softened or it will not blend smoothly with the cream cheese, and will leave lumps.

Don't overheat the white chocolate or the icing will not set.

If the icing has firmed up too much in the fridge, let it sit at room temperature for a few minutes until soft enough to spread.

······················································································

# EASTER SIMNEL CAKE

Traditional simnel cakes can be very deep and quite rich – this one is slightly shallower and lighter. Once you've added the marzipan balls (eleven, for each of the Apostles except Judas) you can decorate further with tiny Easter eggs or fluffy chicks. Tie a yellow or green ribbon around it for the finishing touch.

| Serves 8–10 | PREPARE AHEAD | FREEZE |
|---|---|---|
| | Can be made up to a month ahead and kept, well wrapped, in a cold place. | Freezes well without the marzipan topping. |

FOR THE CAKE

175g (6oz) light muscovado sugar

175g (6oz) butter, softened, plus extra for greasing

175g (6oz) self-raising flour

3 large eggs

50g (2oz) ground almonds

3 tbsp milk

100g (4oz) sultanas

100g (4oz) glacé cherries, washed and quartered (see tip on page 273)

100g (4oz) ready-to-eat dried apricots, snipped into small pieces

2 tsp mixed spice powder

FOR THE TOPPING

450g (1lb) golden marzipan

about 3 tbsp apricot jam

1 egg, beaten

1 You will need a 20cm (8in) round, loose-bottomed cake tin with deep sides. Preheat the oven to 160°C/140°C fan/Gas 3, then grease the tin with butter and line the base with baking paper.

2 Measure all the cake ingredients into a large bowl and beat together well until blended. Spoon half the mixture into the prepared tin and level the surface.

3 Take one-third of the marzipan and roll out into a disc the same size as the base of the cake tin (see tip), then place the disc on top of the cake mixture in the tin. Spoon the remaining cake mixture on top of the marzipan and level the surface.

4 Bake in the oven for 1¾–2 hours or until golden brown on top and firm in the middle. If, towards the end of the cooking time, the cake is getting too brown, cover with a piece of foil. Allow the cake to cool for 10 minutes before removing from the tin (see tip on page 246) and placing on a wire rack to finish cooling.

5 When the cake is cool, heat through the apricot jam in a pan, then brush the top of the cake with a little warm jam. Roll out half the remaining marzipan into a disc to fit the top of the cake (see tip) and place it on top of the layer of jam. Use your thumb to crimp around the edges of the marzipan. Make eleven even-sized balls from the rest of the marzipan and place these around the edge of the cake, spacing them out evenly and fixing them to the marzipan with a little beaten egg.

6 Brush the marzipan with beaten egg and glaze under a hot grill for about 5 minutes (turning the cake round to ensure even browning), so the marzipan is tinged brown all over. (You can also do this with a cook's blowtorch, if you prefer.)

### MARY'S FOOLPROOF TIP

To cut the marzipan to the right size, simply put the cake tin on top of the rolled-out marzipan and cut around it with a sharp knife to make your disc.

# BONFIRE CHOCOLATE TRAYBAKE

This is a light cake, really moist owing to the addition of ground almonds. Being a traybake, it cuts into squares and is so perfect for packing into a box and sharing with family and friends at an event such as Bonfire Night. No icing is needed – just dust with icing sugar to serve, if you like.

Makes 20 squares

PREPARE AHEAD
Can be made up to 2 days ahead.

FREEZE
Freezes well.

225g (8oz) dark chocolate (no more than 40–50% cocoa solids), broken into squares

100g (4oz) butter, cut into small cubes, plus extra for greasing

100g (4oz) caster sugar

3 eggs

75g (3oz) self-raising flour

75g (3oz) ground almonds (see tip)

1 tsp baking powder

1 You will need a 23 x 30cm (9 x 12in) traybake tin. Preheat the oven to 180°C/160°C fan/Gas 4, then line the tin with foil and grease it generously with butter.

2 Place the chocolate and butter in a heatproof bowl set over a pan of hot water and leave until just melted. Once melted, add the sugar and stir to combine, then set aside to cool slightly.

3 Add the eggs, one at a time, to the melted chocolate mixture, beating after each addition. Fold in the flour, ground almonds and baking powder and then pour evenly into the prepared tin.

4 Bake in the oven for 25–30 minutes until the mixture is just set. Allow to cool in the tin before cutting into 20 squares.

## MARY'S FOOLPROOF TIP

Adding ground almonds to a chocolate cake mixture makes it extra moist, which means it keeps well.

# RED VELVET CUPCAKES

These taste as good as they look – moist chocolate sponge with a tangy cream cheese icing. The velvety red colour is obtained from a food-colouring gel, which yields stronger results than a liquid food colouring.

**Makes 12 cupcakes**

**PREPARE AHEAD**
Can be made up to a day ahead and frosted to serve.

**FREEZE**
Freeze well unfrosted.

## FOR THE CUPCAKES
100g (4oz) butter, softened

150g (5oz) caster sugar

125g (4½oz) self-raising flour

25g (1oz) cocoa powder, sifted, plus extra for dusting

2 eggs

2 tbsp milk

10ml (⅓ fl oz) red natural food-colouring gel

## FOR THE FROSTING
50g (2oz) butter, softened

200g (7oz) full-fat cream cheese

300g (11oz) icing sugar, sifted

½ tsp vanilla extract

1 You will need a 12-hole muffin tin and a piping bag fitted with a star nozzle (optional). Preheat the oven to 180°C/160°C fan/Gas 4 and line the tin with paper cases.

2 Measure all the cupcake ingredients into a large bowl and mix together until smooth, either by hand or using an electric hand whisk or food mixer (see tip). Spoon the batter into the paper cases, dividing it evenly between them.

3 Bake in the oven for 20–25 minutes until well risen and springy to the touch. Remove the cupcakes from the tin and leave to cool on a wire rack.

4 To make the frosting, measure all the ingredients into a food processor and whizz until smooth or beat together by hand. Fill the piping bag (if using) with the frosting (see tip) and pipe the frosting on to the cooled cupcakes. Alternatively, add the frosting to the cakes using a teaspoon, spreading it over the top of each cupcake. Dust with cocoa powder to serve.

## MARY'S FOOLPROOF TIPS

If using an electric hand whisk or food mixer to make the sponge, do not over-mix or this may result in flat cakes.

Stand the icing bag in a tall jug with the top of the bag folded over the side to make it easier to fill with the frosting. Make sure the end of the bag is twisted closed as you pipe the frosting on to the cakes so it doesn't leak out.

# FOOLPROOF CAKES

Baking is not only a rewarding and satisfying way to spend an afternoon, especially if sharing the experience with children or grandchildren, but the end results are perfect for serving to friends and family. A homemade treat is guaranteed to prompt smiles and brighten even the dreariest of winter days, and I encourage the young to give their bakes as presents. Whether it's for a picnic, school fete, celebration or simply for restocking the cake tin, there's always an excuse to bake.

BAKING BASICS    Don't let the fact that baking is a science deter you from having a go. Of course, if you're a first-time baker, then start with a simple, classic recipe and if you follow it to the letter, you shouldn't have any problems. In fact, the first rule of baking is to follow the recipe as closely as possible; until you have gained some experience, it's best not to experiment with swapping ingredients or playing with quantities. The other key things to get right are weights, timing, temperature and tin size. If you stick to these simple guidelines, you will get to grips with the basics in no time and are sure to be thrilled with your efforts.

*Timing* Too long in the oven and cakes will overbake, dry out or even burn; not enough time and they will be stodgy and raw. It's tricky to keep track of time, so the safest way to prevent over- or under-baking your cakes is to use a timer.

*Temperature* Baking at the correct temperature is important to guarantee an even rise and texture. Ovens can vary in temperature, so it is worth investing in an oven thermometer if you plan to bake regularly. This will help you gauge the temperature more accurately so that your baking will be more consistent. Remember that when baking in a conventional oven the temperature needs to be 20°C higher than for a fan oven.

*Tin size* Using the right size and shape of tin is essential because cakes will bake at different speeds depending on how shallow or deep the cake mixture is in the tin.

MAKING
AND BAKING
CAKES

DO . . .

***Ensure the oven is preheated*** before you start making your cake. Once the cake mixture is combined, it needs to be baked immediately. Bake on the shelf recommended in your instruction book or recipe.

***Be organised*** Make sure your tin is greased and lined and weigh out all the ingredients before you begin.

***Use softened butter for cakes*** For the creaming method (the beating together of butter and sugar) the butter needs to be soft enough to amalgamate with the sugar easily. It's important to use a finely ground sugar here, such as caster sugar, rather than granulated. For the all-in-one method, you'll need softened butter too. Baking spread can be used straight from the fridge.

*Have patience* Add beaten egg gradually to the creamed butter and sugar mixture, whisking well between each addition. This will help prevent the mixture from curdling.

*Use a metal spoon* whenever the technique of folding is required. Carefully cut and fold the mixture in a figure of eight with your spoon to help prevent air being knocked out of the batter and to ensure the baked sponge is light and airy.

*Divide the cake mixture evenly between tins* If making a sandwich or multi-layered cake using two or more tins, it's important to divide the mixture equally between the tins to ensure the cakes are of a similar size once baked.

*Test for when the cake is done* To do this, insert a fine metal skewer into the middle of the cake – it should come out clean. If there is any mixture stuck to the skewer, return the cake to the oven and check it every 5 minutes until the skewer comes out clean. The cake should be shrinking slightly away from the sides of the tin.

## DON'T . . .

*Try to guess* Baking is a precise science, so it's important to use accurate and reliable scales when weighing out ingredients. Digital scales are the best, particularly those that plug into the mains. It's also well worth investing in some measuring spoons.

*Use ingredients past their expiry date* Raising agents (such as baking powder and bicarbonate of soda), as well as flours, spices and some sugars, have a shelf life, so do check your store cupboard regularly and replace any ingredients that are out of date.

*Over-fill the paper cases* when making cupcakes or muffins. It can be tempting to fill the cases right to the top, but this will cause them to overflow when baking. In general, the cases need to be no more than two-thirds full.

*Open the oven door* until the cake is nearly at the end of the specified baking time, as this will affect the temperature of the oven and disrupt the baking process, which may cause the cake to sink.

## COOLING, ICING AND DECORATING

### DO . . .

*Use a wire rack for cooling* Once your cake has cooled in the tin for a few minutes, carefully remove from the tin. Turn out first on to a clean tea towel, then remove the baking paper from the bottom of the cake and transfer to a wire rack to cool down completely. This prevents the cake from going soggy in the tin. Make sure your cake is completely cold before transferring to an airtight container.

*Ensure butter is soft and icing sugar is sifted* before making a buttercream icing, to guarantee a smooth result.

***Use a piping bag for a more professional finish*** If you want to create a particular pattern, it is easier to use a piping bag and nozzle rather than spreading the icing on the cake with a knife or spoon.

***Choose the correct size of nozzle*** for the effect you are trying to create.

***Stand the piping bag in a tall jug*** with the top hanging over the rim. This makes it easier to fill with icing.

DON'T . . .

***Ice a cake until it is completely cold*** – otherwise the icing will melt in the heat and won't be able to set. Drizzle cakes are the exception here: the cake needs to be warm when the sugar syrup/glaze is added so that it can seep evenly into the sponge.

***Over-fill a piping bag with icing*** This can cause the heat from your hands to warm up the icing, making it the wrong consistency and trickier to work with.

***Add liquid all at once when making glacé icing*** Add the liquid to the sifted icing sugar in stages until you achieve the right consistency. It's easy to add too much and end up with an icing that's too liquid – better to include too little initially as you can always add more if needed.

# CHOCOLATE AND CHERRY BISCUITS

**Based on a fork biscuit, one of the easiest types of biscuit to make, these have added texture from the lovely chewy glacé cherries in the dough and studding the tops.**

Makes 16 biscuits

PREPARE AHEAD
Can be made up to 4 days ahead and kept in an airtight container.

FREEZE
Freeze well cooked.

100g (4oz) butter, softened

50g (2oz) caster sugar

125g (4½oz) self-raising flour

15g (½oz) cocoa powder

75g (3oz) glacé cherries, chopped, plus 8 glacé cherries, halved, to decorate

icing sugar, for dusting

1 Preheat the oven to 180°C/160°C fan/Gas 4 and line two baking sheets with baking paper.

2 Measure the butter and caster sugar into a bowl and beat with a wooden spoon until combined. Add the flour, cocoa powder and the chopped cherries. Mix together with the spoon and then bring together with your hands to form a dough.

3 Divide into 16 even-sized balls. Arrange eight, spaced well apart, on each of the prepared baking sheets and then flatten each ball of dough by pressing down with the back of a wet fork until about 1cm (½in) thick.

4 Bake in the oven for 12–15 minutes until just cooked – taking care as they become dark very easily. Remove from the oven and immediately press a cherry half into the centre of each biscuit (see tip), then allow to cool for 5 minutes on the baking sheets before transferring to a wire rack to cool down fully and firm up.

5 Once cold, dust with icing sugar to serve.

## MARY'S FOOLPROOF TIP

Each biscuit needs to be warm for the cherry half to embed into it. The cherries for decoration should still have their sticky syrup on them so they stick to the warm biscuits. Once the biscuits are cold, the cherries will be set firm.

# GINGER AND WHITE CHOCOLATE FLORENTINES

**These impressive biscuits are smart enough to serve with coffee after a dinner party or to accompany a chilled dessert.**

| Makes 16 biscuits | PREPARE AHEAD<br>Can be made up to 2 days ahead. | FREEZE<br>Freeze well cooked but without the icing. |
| --- | --- | --- |

50g (2oz) butter

50g (2oz) golden syrup

50g (2oz) demerara sugar

50g (2oz) plain flour

50g (2oz) shelled pistachios, chopped

50g (2oz) stem ginger in syrup, drained and chopped

200g (7oz) good-quality white chocolate (see tip on page 221), broken into squares

**1** Preheat the oven to 180°C/160°C fan/Gas 4 and line two baking sheets with baking paper.

**2** Measure the butter, golden syrup and sugar into a saucepan and melt over a medium heat, stirring until the butter has melted and the sugar has dissolved.

**3** Add the flour, pistachios and ginger, and stir to mix until combined. Using a teaspoon, spoon blobs of the Florentine batter on to the prepared baking sheets, spacing them well apart as they will spread a little during cooking.

**4** Bake in the oven for 8–10 minutes until golden and cooked through. Leave to cool for a few minutes, then use a palette knife to carefully transfer them to a wire rack to cool down fully and set firm.

**5** Place the white chocolate in a heatproof bowl set over a pan of hot water. Stir until melted and smooth, taking great care not to let the chocolate get too hot – it should just be lukewarm (see tip). Set aside to cool down to room temperature and thicken to a coating consistency (see tip).

**6** Use a pastry brush to paint one side of each Florentine with white chocolate, or dip half of each biscuit into the melted chocolate and smooth over with a fork. Leave to set on the wire rack before serving.

## MARY'S FOOLPROOF TIPS

Do not overheat the white chocolate as it will split and be too runny for dipping the Florentines.

Let the chocolate cool down, stirring occasionally, to room temperature. It needs to have thickened so that it will coat the Florentines well. Any warmer and it will be too thin and just run off the biscuits when transferred to the wire rack.

# TWO-TONE TOFFEE CHEWS

This is an updated version of a recipe I first made 40 years ago. Naughty to eat and so easy to make, children will love them – my daughter Annabel still makes them now with her children. It is a fun – and delicious! – way to use up a packet of marshmallows or toffees.

Makes 48 squares

PREPARE AHEAD
Can be made up to 4 days ahead and kept in an airtight tin.

225g (8oz)
  marshmallows
225g (8oz)
  butter toffees
225g (8oz) butter
175g (6oz) crisped
  rice cereal
175g (6oz) chocolate
  crisped rice cereal

1 You will need a 23 x 30cm (9 x 12in) traybake tin. Grease the tin with butter and line the base with baking paper.

2 Measure the marshmallows, toffees and butter into a very large, non-stick saucepan and heat gently, stirring from time to time, until they have all melted and combined (see tip).

3 Remove from the heat, add the crisped rice cereals and stir to combine. Tip the mixture into the prepared tin and level the top with the back of a spoon. Transfer to the fridge to chill for at least an hour.

4 Once firm, run a knife round the edge of the tin and cut across the tin 6 x 8 to make 48 squares.

## MARY'S FOOLPROOF TIP

Make sure all the ingredients are melted before adding the crisped rice cereals. The butter will melt first, then the marshmallows, and the toffee last. Stir vigorously to combine everything and make sure the lumps of toffee have melted.

# SWEET LEMON CRISPS

These are for when you are in a mad rush and have no time to make biscuits – a delicious cheat!
Great to serve with mousse, ice cream or coffee.

Makes 24 crisps

**PREPARE AHEAD**
Can be made up to 3 days ahead and
stored in an airtight box (see tip).

**FREEZE**
Freeze well cooked.

½ x 375g packet
  of ready-rolled,
  all-butter puff pastry
1 egg white, beaten
finely grated zest
  of 1 lemon
50g (2oz) caster sugar

**1** Roll out the pastry between two large pieces of cling film, rolling as thinly as
you can and to about 35cm (14in) square. Try to get the pastry super-thin and
even, like a sheet of paper. Remove the top piece of cling film.

**2** Brush the pastry with the beaten egg white and sprinkle evenly with the lemon
zest and sugar.

**3** Cut the pastry into two rows of three rectangles (each about 10 x 15cm/4 x 6in)
and then cut diagonally across each rectangle to make an 'X'. You will end up
with 24 triangles.

**4** Using a palette knife, transfer the pieces of pastry very carefully to the prepared
baking sheet, spacing each triangle well apart. Chill in the fridge for 15 minutes.
While the pastry is chilling, preheat the oven to 200°C/180°C fan/Gas 6 and line
a large baking sheet with baking paper.

5 Bake in the oven for 10–12 minutes until golden and crisp. Transfer to a wire
rack and leave to cool completely before serving.

## MARY'S FOOLPROOF TIPS

Layer in an airtight plastic box with kitchen paper in between each layer to keep
them fresh.

For a change, you can shape these like cheese straws and serve them standing up
in a scoop of ice cream.

# CRANBERRY AND COCONUT ENERGY BARS

Do you remember those crisped rice cakes in chocolate or golden syrup that we used to make in paper cases? These are the fruity version – with no baking required! Indeed, you could make these in 30 paper cases if you preferred. They are great for a packed lunch or eating on the go.

Makes 18 bars

**PREPARE AHEAD**
Can be made up to 3 days ahead.

200g (7oz)
  butter, softened
200g (7oz) light
  muscovado sugar
100g (4oz)
  golden syrup
50g (2oz)
  sunflower seeds
50g (2oz) dried
  cranberries,
  chopped if large
100g (4oz) sultanas
50g (2oz)
  desiccated coconut
100g (4oz) crisped
  rice cereal
150g (5oz)
  rolled oats

1 Line a 23 x 30cm (9 x 12in) traybake tin with cling film (see tip on page 58).

2 Measure the butter, sugar and golden syrup into a large saucepan and stir over a medium heat until melted. Pour into a large bowl, stir in all the remaining ingredients and mix well until combined and coated.

3 Tip into the prepared tin and spread with the back of a spoon into an even layer. Transfer to the fridge to chill for about 2 hours until firm (see tip).

4 Cut into 18 even-sized bars and keep in an airtight container until needed.

## MARY'S FOOLPROOF TIP

Chilling the mixture is so important, as it makes the bars much easier to cut.

# STEM GINGER SHORTBREAD

To me shortbread is the ultimate biscuit – a favourite in every way. I serve these each week after a game of tennis with my girlfriends – we chat more than we play, I have to admit, but it is fun and helps keep me fit!

| Makes 30 fingers or triangles | PREPARE AHEAD | FREEZE |
| --- | --- | --- |
| | Can be made up to 3 days ahead and kept in an airtight container in between layers of kitchen paper to prevent them from sticking together | The cooked shortbread freezes well. Refresh in a moderate oven for about 10 minutes (no need to defrost first). |

5 balls of stem ginger in syrup, drained and finely chopped

225g (8oz) plain flour, plus extra for dusting

225g (8oz) butter

100g (4oz) caster sugar

100g (4oz) semolina

2 tbsp demerara sugar

1 You will need a 23 x 33cm (9 x 13in) traybake tin. Preheat the oven to 160°C/140°C fan/Gas 3.

2 Dry the chopped ginger thoroughly with kitchen paper to absorb all the excess syrup.

3 Measure the flour, butter, caster sugar and semolina into a large bowl and rub together with your fingertips, or whizz in a food processor for a few minutes, until the mixture comes together in a very crumbly dough (see tip). Tip on to a lightly floured worktop and knead in the chopped ginger.

4 Press the dough into the traybake tin and, using the back of a spoon, level the surface. Sprinkle with the demerara sugar, then bake in the oven for 40 minutes or until very pale golden and firm to the touch.

5 Leave to cool for 5 minutes, then cut the shortbread into 30 even-sized fingers or triangles (see tip). Carefully remove from the tin (see tip) and transfer to a wire rack to cool completely.

## MARY'S FOOLPROOF TIPS

The mixture is very crumbly – a dry dough rather than a smooth pastry.

To make shortbread triangles, cut 5 x 3 lines across the tin and slice each square in half diagonally to give 30 triangles.

You must remove the biscuits from the tin as soon as they have been cut and just cooled, or they will stick to the tin.

# SHREWSBURY BISCUITS

**I love this classic biscuit with its delicate buttery flavour offset by the currants and lemon zest. Perfect for a snack at any time of day.**

Makes 24 biscuits

PREPARE AHEAD
Can be made up to 3 days ahead and kept in an airtight container.

FREEZE
Freeze the dough after kneading. Defrost at room temperature.

100g (4oz) butter, softened

75g (3oz) caster sugar, plus extra for dusting

1 egg, separated

finely grated zest of 1 small lemon

200g (7oz) plain flour, plus extra for dusting

50g (2oz) currants

1–2 tbsp milk

1 You will need a 6cm (2½in) fluted pastry cutter. Preheat the oven to 200°C/180°C fan/Gas 6 and line two baking sheets with baking paper.

2 Measure the butter and sugar into a large bowl and cream together until pale and fluffy, either by hand or with an electric hand whisk. Add the egg yolk and lemon zest, sift in the flour and mix well to combine. Add the currants and 1 tablespoon of the milk and mix with the blade of a round-ended table knife to give a fairly soft dough, adding more milk if needed. When it starts to come together, use your hands to bring it into a ball (see tip).

3 Knead the dough on a lightly floured work surface (see tip) and, using a rolling pin, roll out the dough to about 5mm (¼in) thick. Use the pastry cutter to stamp out 24 discs from the dough (see tip), re-rolling it as necessary. Lift each disc with a palette knife and place on the prepared baking sheets.

4 Bake the biscuits in the oven for about 8 minutes and, while they are cooking, lightly beat the egg white with a fork until frothy. Remove the biscuits and brush the tops with the beaten egg white. Sprinkle over some extra caster sugar and return to the oven for a further 5 minutes or until pale golden and cooked through.

5 Leave to cool on the baking sheets for a few minutes, then use the palette knife to carefully lift the biscuits on to a wire rack to cool completely.

## MARY'S FOOLPROOF TIPS

Work quickly in a cool area of the kitchen so the dough doesn't soften. If it is soft after mixing, chill in the fridge for about 10 minutes until easier to handle.

When rolling out the dough, be sparing with the flour used to dust the surface, otherwise the dough will take it up and become too dry and crack.

When cutting out the biscuits, try not to twist or wiggle the cutter in the dough, as you want to achieve a nice fluted edge to each biscuit.

# HOT CROSS BUNS

An Easter classic that's loved by all, these are best made and eaten on the day.
They are delicious split in half and spread with butter.

Makes 12 buns

FREEZE
Freeze well for up to a month.

500g (1lb 2oz)
  strong white flour,
  plus extra for dusting
75g (3oz) caster sugar
2 tsp mixed spice powder
1 tsp ground cinnamon
finely grated zest
  of 1 lemon
10g (½oz) salt
10g (½oz) fast-action
  dried yeast
40g (1½oz) butter
about 300ml (10fl oz)
  milk
1 egg, beaten
200g (7oz) sultanas
50g (2oz) finely
  chopped mixed peel
oil, for greasing

FOR THE TOPPING
75g (3oz) plain flour
2 tbsp golden syrup,
  for glazing

**1** You will need a piping bag fitted with a fine 3mm (⅛in) nozzle (see tip).

**2** Measure the flour, sugar and spices into a large bowl, add the lemon zest and toss together, then add the salt and yeast, placing them on opposite sides of the bowl.

**3** Melt the butter in a pan and warm the milk in a separate pan, allowing them both to cool a little after heating. Add the melted butter and half the tepid milk to the dry ingredients in the bowl. Tip in the beaten egg and use your hands to bring the mixture together, incorporating the flour from the edges of the bowl as you go. Gradually add the rest of the milk, to make a soft pliable dough. You may not need all the milk – it is better for the dough to be on the wet side, rather than too dry.

**4** Tip the dough out on to a lightly floured work surface and knead by hand, incorporating the sultanas and mixed peel into the dough. Lightly knead for 10 minutes until silky and elastic and forming a smooth ball (see tip).

**5** Transfer the ball of dough into an oiled bowl, cover with cling film and leave to rise in a warm place for about 1½ hours or until doubled in size. (This may take longer if the dough is left to rise in a cool kitchen.)

**6** Turn the risen dough out on to a lightly floured surface. Knock back and knead for a further 5 minutes. Return to the bowl, cover with cling film and leave in a warm place to rise for a further hour, or until doubled in size.

**7** Turn the dough out again on to a floured surface and divide into 12 equal pieces, shaping each of these into a ball. Line 1–2 baking sheets with baking paper and arrange the balls of dough on the sheets, placing them fairly close together and flattening them slightly.

**8** Slip each baking sheet into a large, clean polythene bag, making sure that the bag doesn't touch the buns. Leave for 40–60 minutes until the buns have doubled in size. They should spring back when lightly pressed with a finger. Meanwhile, preheat the oven to 220°C/200°C fan/Gas 7.

**9** To make the crosses for the top of the buns, add the plain flour to a bowl with 100ml (3½fl oz) of water. Mix together to make a paste and spoon into the piping bag (if using).

**10** When the buns have risen, remove the polythene bags and pipe a cross on top of each bun. Transfer the buns to the oven and bake for 15–20 minutes until pale golden brown, turning the baking sheets round halfway through, if necessary.

**11** Melt the golden syrup in a pan and, while the buns are still warm, brush the top of each bun with a little melted syrup to give a nice shine, before setting aside to cool on a wire rack.

## MARY'S FOOLPROOF TIPS

If you don't have a piping bag with a nozzle, use a disposable piping bag instead and carefully snip the end off. You can also make crosses from two strips of thinly rolled-out shortcrust pastry, if you prefer.

Kneading can be done in a food mixer using a dough hook, if you prefer.

# THE
# FOOLPROOF
# KITCHEN

# THE FOOLPROOF STORE CUPBOARD

If you cook regularly and are keen to expand your repertoire, a well-stocked store cupboard and fridge will make it much easier for you to vary your cooking and to experiment with recipes, without feeling the need to take a shopping trip each time you want to try something new.

Of course, I'm not suggesting you go out and buy a whole range of obscure ingredients only for them to be used once and then hidden away at the back of a cupboard. Rather, you should ensure you have the basics to make everyday cooking less of a chore, plus a few handy extras up your sleeve to enable you to transform an ordinary dish into something special. Having a good selection of ingredients at your fingertips will also make you less likely to get stuck in a rut and keep you better equipped for making a wider variety of delicious recipes.

|  | THE BASICS *Essentials for a well-stocked store cupboard* | | A LITTLE EXTRA *Star ingredients to enhance your cooking* | |
| --- | --- | --- | --- | --- |
| BAKING | Plain and self-raising flour  Baking powder and bicarbonate of soda  **Sugar** caster and icing sugar  Runny honey | Eggs  Cocoa powder  Ground almonds  Vanilla extract  Almond extract  Rolled oats | **Chocolate** good-quality white, dark and milk  Fast-action dried yeast  Strong flour for bread-making | **Brown sugar** dark and light muscovado, demerara  Golden syrup  Maple syrup |
| NUTS, SEEDS AND DRIED FRUIT | **Almonds** whole blanched, flaked  Sesame seeds | Raisins and sultanas  Dried apricots | **Coconut** desiccated and flakes  Pistachios  Hazelnuts | Sunflower and pumpkin seeds  Dried cranberries, figs, dates, currants |
| SPICES, HERBS AND SEASONINGS | **Salt** table and coarse sea salt  **Stock cubes** chicken, vegetable and beef  Peppercorns  **Ground spices** cumin, coriander, cinnamon, ginger, nutmeg, turmeric, chilli powder, mixed spice, paprika, | sweet smoked paprika, black pepper  **Whole spices** cardamom pods, cinnamon sticks, star anise  **Spice blends** garam masala, curry powder, Chinese five-spice powder  **Dried herbs** bay leaves | **Whole spices** nutmeg; cumin, coriander, mustard and fennel seeds; dried chillies, cinnamon sticks | **Ground spices** cayenne pepper, za'atar spice blend |

| | THE BASICS<br>*Essentials for a well-stocked store cupboard* | | A LITTLE EXTRA<br>*Star ingredients to enhance your cooking* | |
| --- | --- | --- | --- | --- |
| OILS | Olive oil and extra-virgin olive oil | Sunflower oil<br>Sesame oil | | |
| VINEGARS | White wine vinegar<br>Red wine vinegar | Balsamic vinegar<br>Rice vinegar | Cider vinegar | |
| CONDIMENTS | Tomato ketchup<br>Tomato purée<br>Worcestershire sauce<br>Yeast extract<br>Soy sauce<br>Thai fish sauce<br>Redcurrant jelly | **Mustard**<br>English, Dijon, wholegrain, powder<br>**Curry pastes**<br>Thai and Indian<br>Good-quality mayonnaise | Harissa paste<br>Sun-dried tomato paste | Tamarind paste<br>Horseradish sauce |
| TINNED AND PRESERVED FOODS | Anchovies<br>Tuna<br>Capers<br>Chopped tomatoes<br>Tomato passata<br>Chickpeas<br>Sun-dried tomatoes | **Beans**<br>butter beans, cannellini and kidney beans<br>Olives<br>Ready-roasted peppers<br>Coconut milk | Flageolet beans<br>Sweetcorn<br>Sun-blushed tomatoes<br>Dried porcini mushrooms | Preserved lemons<br>Full-fat condensed milk<br>Borlotti beans |
| GRAINS AND PULSES | Couscous<br>Red lentils | Puy lentils | Quinoa | Bulghur wheat |
| PASTA, NOODLES AND RICE | Linguine or spaghetti<br>Penne and other shapes<br>**Small pasta**<br>such as orzo<br>Egg noodles | **Basmati rice**<br>white or brown<br>Parboiled rice<br>Risotto rice<br>Pudding rice | Wild rice<br>Jasmine rice<br>Soba and rice noodles | |
| FOR THE FRIDGE | Milk<br>Eggs<br>Butter<br>Baking spread | Double cream | **Cheese**<br>Parmesan, Cheddar, a blue cheese and a full-fat cream cheese | Streaky bacon or pancetta |

# THE FOOLPROOF FREEZER

Essential to any kitchen, the freezer offers multi-purpose storage, allowing you to keep useful ingredients for midweek family meals, prepare dishes ahead for entertaining and help prevent waste by enabling you to store leftover portions or ingredients. Keeping an efficiently run freezer can save you time, money and hassle. Follow these foolproof tips to get the most out of your freezer.

## WHAT CAN YOU FREEZE

### VEGETABLES, HERBS, SPICES AND NUTS

*Vegetables* Frozen vegetables are a brilliant standby and will help you stick to a healthy diet even when time is short. Most vegetables can be frozen (except those with a particularly high water content – see page 308). Cook first in boiling water for 1–3 minutes, then drain and plunge straight into ice-cold water to halt the cooking process. Frozen vegetables should be cooked from frozen, rather than defrosted first.

*Herbs* Most herbs can be frozen: chop and freeze in ice-cube trays topped up with a little water. Softer herbs are better made into a pesto or a herb butter before freezing (see page 308). For chives, take a bundle of long stems, tie with string at both ends and wrap in foil. To use, snip off fine pieces from the frozen bundle, then return to the freezer.

*Ginger, chilli and garlic* Knobs of root ginger can be frozen, wrapped in cling film, and then grated from frozen. Chillies should be chopped before freezing; they can also be used straight from the freezer as they will defrost almost instantly. Peel garlic cloves before freezing, then grate straight from frozen.

*Curry leaves, Kaffir lime leaves and bay leaves* can all be frozen – ready to add authentic flavour to curries, soups and casseroles.

*Shelled and ground nuts* Whole nuts keep well for 3 years, ground for 1 year. I find it is always useful to have flaked almonds, ground almonds and chestnuts.

### MEAT AND FISH

*Raw meat and fish* freeze well. Always make sure it is as fresh as possible and well wrapped and don't keep it for longer than 3 months. After this time it is edible but the quality will deteriorate. Label well with the cut, meat and date, as once frozen, meats can look very similar!

*Cooked meat* can also be frozen. Ensure it is completely cold before freezing.

### FRUIT

Most fruit freezes very well and is excellent to have on standby for making an impromptu pud. Berries – such as raspberries, blackberries, blackcurrants, gooseberries, redcurrants and blueberries – should be frozen in a single layer on a tray until solid and then decanted into a freezer bag; this will prevent them from being squashed or damaged. Soft fruits such as strawberries and peaches will turn mushy on freezing, so it's best to purée them first. Apples, rhubarb, plums and cherries are best sliced up and stewed with a little sugar before freezing.

## MAIN COURSES

Being able to get ahead by freezing a main course for a dinner party is invaluable. Many cooked and cooled dishes, such as casseroles, bakes, gratins, fishcakes and soups, can be frozen. I often double up a recipe when I'm cooking in order to have one to eat straight away and one to freeze for a later date.

## DESSERTS & PUDDINGS

Many puddings can be frozen, which is a huge help if you're planning a party or getting ahead for Christmas. Roulades, cheesecakes and pastry-based desserts are among those that can be frozen – always refer to the recipe for how best to do this. In general, it's best to open-freeze until solid in order to prevent damage, then wrap well and freeze until needed.

## CAKES, BISCUITS AND PASTRY

*Raw cookie and biscuit dough* freezes very well. Freeze it in a log shape, ready to defrost, then slice into rounds to bake.

*Raw pastry* freezes well. If you're getting ahead for a dinner party, it can be easier to freeze a made-up pastry case than a block of raw pastry. Pastry cases that have been baked blind can also be frozen, though they can become more fragile to handle.

*Unfrosted, baked cakes* freeze well and it's so useful to have a sweet treat ready to whip out for a special occasion. Ensure your cake is completely cold after baking, then wrap in a double layer of cling film to protect against freezer burn. Allow 3–4 hours to defrost at room temperature, depending on the cake's size. Icing it to serve makes it look fresh.

*Baked biscuits and cookies* can be frozen; pack them snugly in a container layered with kitchen paper to reduce the amount of air around them (see page 308).

## MILK, CREAM, BUTTER AND CHEESE

*Milk* It is handy to keep a pint of homogenized milk in the freezer; defrost in a sink of cold water and shake well before use.

*Double cream and clotted cream* freeze well for up to 3 months because of their high fat content. Double cream does become a little thick on thawing.

*Butter and hard cheese* (such as Parmesan and Cheddar) can be frozen. It's useful to grate hard cheese before freezing, however, as this will defrost more quickly. Leftover rich cheeses like camembert and blue cheese should be wrapped well.

### EGGS

*Raw egg whites and yolks* can be frozen separately. This is really useful if you have made a meringue or custard and have some separated egg white or yolk left over. Ensure you make a note of quantity on the label.

*Cooked eggs* do not freeze well; they become rubbery in texture.

### BREAD

Keeping a loaf or two in the freezer is an essential standby. Ready-sliced bread can be toasted straight from frozen. Allow a couple of hours for whole loaves to defrost.

## WHAT YOU CAN'T FREEZE

*Raw meat and fish that has already been frozen* As a general rule, it's best not to refreeze anything that has already been frozen before, as the quality will deteriorate. But if it is in perfect condition going into the freezer, it should be safe when thawed.

*Salad ingredients* The water content of most salad (such as tomatoes, lettuce and cucumber) is too high to freeze; they would turn mushy on defrosting.

*Fresh, soft herbs* – such as basil, coriander and dill. These are too delicate to freeze as they are, but you can whizz them into a pesto or make a herb butter (by adding them to softened butter) before freezing.

*Low-fat dairy products* – such as yoghurt, single cream and cream cheese. These turn watery and separate on defrosting.

*Egg-based sauces* such as hollandaise or mayonnaise cannot be frozen as they will separate on defrosting.

*Pavlova and meringue* There is no need to freeze pavlova or cooked meringues as they keep in an airtight container in a cool place for up to 2 months. Stored in the freezer, they become too brittle and can be damaged easily.

## PREPARING FOOD FOR THE FREEZER

### DO . . .

*Ensure food is cold* Cooked food needs to be completely cold before it can be frozen, to ensure food safety.

*Double-wrap food to protect against freezer burn* Freezing can be harsh on certain foods, so double-wrap in foil or cling film or use plastic freezer bags to help prevent foods from being damaged.

*Leave space for expansion* Don't forget that liquids expand on freezing, so take care not to fill containers or freezer bags all the way to the top when adding soups, stocks or purées for freezing. Leave a little space to allow the liquid to expand.

*Use the correct size of container* When freezing cooked solid food or leftovers, it's important to decant it into an appropriate-sized container to ensure minimal air surrounds the food; too much space will cause it to dry out during freezing. If using freezer bags, ensure that you squeeze out as much air as possible.

## DON'T . . .

*Freeze food that is past its best* If you're thinking of freezing something because you don't want to waste it but you know it's no longer fresh, it really isn't worth it as the food won't improve on freezing – once defrosted, it will be in exactly the same condition as it was before freezing.

## KEEPING AN ORGANISED FREEZER

### DO . . .

*Label and date* everything that goes into the freezer. You'll be able to find what you're looking for much more easily, less likely to forget what you have or leave it in the freezer too long. Write down the number of servings and any reheating instructions.

*Group together foods* Aim to keep the same types of foods together by allocating them to different shelves or drawers – store meat and fish in one drawer, for instance, and cakes, biscuits and desserts together in another drawer.

*Keep a list* of exactly what is in the freezer and the date it was frozen. This will help you to keep tabs on what needs using up; it will also make meal planning easier if you know what you already have. Make sure you keep it up to date by crossing things off the list when you have used them (I have yet to perfect this, but I'm improving!).

### DON'T . . .

*Freeze anything for longer than 4 months* Many foods can be kept in the freezer for up to 6 months, but their flavour and quality will deteriorate over time, so it's best to keep track of how long things have been kept so that you can enjoy them at their best. Aim to tidy your freezer every 2 months so that you can see what needs to be used up. Put it all into one shelf so that you are reminded to use it.

## DEFROSTING AND REHEATING

As a general rule, every recipe from this book should be defrosted in the fridge before cooking, unless stated otherwise.

### DO . . .

*Defrost in a cool place* Ideally all food (and especially meat and fish) should be defrosted slowly in the fridge. This is less important for bread, cakes and biscuits, which can be thawed at room temperature.

*Allow plenty of time* Large joints of meat and whole birds can take up to 2 days to defrost completely, so ensure you plan ahead.

*Reheat thoroughly* It is crucial that meat, fish and poultry dishes are reheated until piping hot all the way through. They should reach boiling point for 10 minutes in the centre (or for 3–4 minutes if cooking in the microwave) and be fully cooked to prevent any risk of food poisoning.

### DON'T . . .

*Cheat* Trying to rush thawing can be dangerous and could result in food poisoning.

# FOOLPROOF FAMILY FOOD

Preparing a tasty and nutritious family meal when you're short of time and on a budget can be a challenge for even the most experienced of home cooks. Indeed, with so many pressures on you during the week it's not easy to maintain the enthusiasm for cooking. With this is mind, I've put together a few tips and tricks to help you be as efficient as possible and hopefully make the task of everyday cooking a little easier.

**GETTING ORGANISED**

*Try to have a well-stocked store cupboard* (see page 304) so that on days when things don't go according to plan, you can still whip up a quick supper without having to trek to the shops.

*Plan weekday meals* If you can plan your evening meals in advance, this will take away the pressure and panic of having to think up something on the day.

*Invest time in batch cooking and freeze ahead* When you're preparing a casserole, soup or stew, it's worth making extra so that you can freeze portions to eat at a later date, ready to defrost on days when time is short. Make a note in your diary as a reminder that you have a dish in the freezer.

**WHEN TIME IS SHORT**

Time is often the trickiest part of cooking for a family, especially during the week. If you have a well-stocked store cupboard, fridge and freezer, however, you should be able to whip up a nutritious supper in a matter of minutes. Here are just a few suggestions:

DO . . .

*Remember the wok (or large non-stick frying pan)* Stir-fries are a great option for a quick supper and can be a healthy choice too. Once the vegetables are chopped, a stir-fry can be ready in under 10 minutes. Keep a bag of large peeled prawns in the freezer and add some straight-to-wok noodles to make your stir-fry more substantial.

*Use short cuts* Don't be afraid to use 'cheat's' ingredients if you're short of time. A fantastic range of ready-made ingredients is now available, which can dramatically reduce cooking time. Tinned beans, ready-rolled pastry, instant grains and curry pastes are all excellent time-saving store-cupboard must-haves for midweek cooking.

DON'T . . .

*Forget about eggs* They are brilliantly versatile, filling, healthy and quick to prepare. Omelettes and frittatas are both excellent meals – ready in minutes and easy to adapt depending on whatever leftovers you have in the fridge.

## WHEN YOU'RE ON A BUDGET

Cooking on a tight budget isn't easy, but if you follow my simple guidelines you should be able to rustle up some good-value, healthy and flavoursome meals.

DO . . .

*Eat seasonal fruit and vegetables* It's much cheaper to buy fruit and vegetables when they are abundant and in season.

*Use frozen vegetables* These tend to have just as many nutrients as fresh vegetables, and have the added advantage of no longer being perishable once frozen, so they are a good option if you're trying to cut down on waste.

*Buy British, and local if you can* In general, home-grown produce is less expensive than exotic fruit and vegetables because it costs less to transport.

*Eat less meat* Meat and fish are expensive and we don't need to eat them every day. So long as you ensure that there are good sources of protein within your diet, it is not necessary to eat meat and fish daily.

*Get to grips with grains and pulses* Beans, lentils, grains and seeds are all valuable sources of vegetarian protein and are very good value for money. Incorporating more of these into your weekly meals will help shave pennies off your food bill.

*Choose cheaper cuts of meat* Cuts such as shoulder of lamb, minced meat or braising steak are much cheaper than prime cuts of meat and with careful slow cooking can be easily transformed into delicious family meals without too much expense.

*Plan your meals* This will help avoid any unnecessary waste and should mean that you use up ingredients before needing to buy new ones.

*Make the most of your freezer* Keeping tabs on what is in the freezer and how long it has been there (see page 306) will help you plan efficiently and prevent waste.

*Shop locally* Getting to know your local shops and shopkeepers is helpful as they can share their knowledge of what cuts and ingredients are cheaper, or what's in season.

DON'T . . .

*Throw away leftovers* Eat them for lunch the next day, freeze any leftover portions or combine them with other ingredients to transform them into another dish.

*Discard slightly stale bread* Whizz it into breadcrumbs and freeze for when you need crumbs for meat, fish or gratins.

*Bin overripe fruit and vegetables* Most of these can be salvaged. Overripe bananas are perfect for making banana bread, for instance: simply freeze in their skins until you have time to bake. Overripe tomatoes are ideal for making a tomato sauce or soup or for adding to stews. Overripe berries can be whizzed with other fruit into breakfast smoothies or juices.

*Be ruled by sell-by dates* It is the 'use by' or 'best before' dates that you need to watch to ensure food is not past its best. While it's important to take note of these dates for meat, fish and dairy produce, where vegetables and fruit are concerned it is easy to determine whether the produce is still edible, regardless of the date on the packaging.

# FOOLPROOF ENTERTAINING

Do you find entertaining stressful? The timing, the presentation and the pressure to impress are all things that can make it less enjoyable, but with a little practice and by sticking to a few simple guidelines you will be able to enjoy the preparations and have as much fun as your guests.

The key to foolproof entertaining lies in planning and preparation. I'm a firm believer in preparing ahead as much as possible so that you can avoid any last-minute hassle. Whether you're planning a kitchen supper, Sunday roast or special celebration, it's essential that you invest time in forward planning to ensure the event goes as smoothly as possible.

CHOOSING WHAT TO COOK

This is the first, and often trickiest, hurdle to cross when having people round. Selecting different courses for your meal is important, as you want to pick a menu that is well balanced and impressive yet not too time-consuming or complex to prepare. The ideal menu for a keen cook is one that is challenging enough to be rewarding but not so over-ambitious as to cause stress.

*Begin by choosing your main course* This is the main part of the meal and so it makes sense to decide on this first and then plan the rest of the menu around it.

*Consider what is in season and the time of year* Seasonal ingredients tend to be better value for money. If the weather is freezing cold, then opt for a warming and comforting menu rather than something refreshing and light that would be better suited to a summer meal.

*Think about numbers* If you are cooking for a large number of guests, you may want to select a simpler menu with fewer dishes. You may also want to choose dishes with less expensive ingredients, as these can add up considerably when you are cooking for a crowd.

*Check about allergies and special diets* It's important to find out whether your guests have any special dietary requirements, so that you can tailor the menu accordingly.

*Think about colour and texture* Try to choose dishes that complement each other in terms of texture, colour and flavour. It's always preferable to have a variety of textures and colours on a plate.

*Avoid repetition* If you have a pastry tart for a starter, for instance, you will want to avoid pastry in the rest of the menu. Similarly, if you have a creamy dessert in mind, you should avoid a rich creamy sauce with the main course, as this would make the menu too heavy.

**FORWARD PLANNING AND GETTING ORGANISED**

***Choose dishes that can be prepared ahead*** If you're cooking for a crowd, try to choose cold or frozen desserts that can be prepared at least a day in advance (see page 307). Opt for a couple of cold side dishes that can also be prepared ahead. Having cold side dishes and a chilled dessert frees up more time to spend on the main dish.

***Keep it simple*** It's easy to get carried away and stretch yourself too much. Remember that you only have one pair of hands, so it's better to make a success of a smaller number of dishes rather than over-stretch yourself with too many.

***Make a time plan*** Write a list of everything you have to do for each dish and then plan out the order in which to do them to make the best use of the time you have.

***Check equipment*** Make sure you have everything you need for the recipes before you start cooking.

***Check serving dishes and utensils*** This is especially important if you're serving a buffet for a large party. You need to make sure you have enough large platters, bowls and appropriate serving utensils for the number of dishes you are making.

***Get ahead*** It's best to do as much preparation as you can ahead of time so that you are not rushed off your feet on the day.

***Clear fridge space*** – as much as you can before a large party. You will need plenty of space for ingredients as well as the dishes that are being prepared in advance.

***Delegate*** Ask any willing volunteers to help with setting the table, organising drinks and general tidying before the party.

***Remember the drinks!*** Wine, beer and soft drinks will all need to be chilled ahead of the event, so ensure you leave enough time and clear enough space in the fridge. If you're hosting a large party, remember that you can hire glasses from many supermarkets or wine merchants if you don't have enough at home. And don't forget to stock up on ice!

# CONVERSION TABLES

## MEASUREMENTS

| METRIC | IMPERIAL |
|--------|----------|
| 5mm | ¼in |
| 1cm | ½in |
| 2.5cm | 1in |
| 5cm | 2in |
| 8cm | 3in |
| 10cm | 4in |
| 12.5cm | 5in |
| 15cm | 6in |
| 18cm | 7in |
| 20cm | 8in |
| 23cm | 9in |
| 25cm | 10in |
| 30cm | 12in |

## OVEN TEMPERATURES

| °C | °C FAN | °F | GAS MARK |
|------|-----------|--------|----------|
| 140°C | 120°C fan | 275°F | Gas 1 |
| 150°C | 130°C fan | 300°F | Gas 2 |
| 160°C | 140°C fan | 325°F | Gas 3 |
| 180°C | 160°C fan | 350°F | Gas 4 |
| 190°C | 170°C fan | 375°F | Gas 5 |
| 200°C | 180°C fan | 400°F | Gas 6 |
| 220°C | 200°C fan | 425°F | Gas 7 |
| 230°C | 210°C fan | 450°F | Gas 8 |
| 240°C | 220°C fan | 475°F | Gas 9 |

Both metric and imperial measures are provided – always follow one or the other, never mix the two.

Spoon measures throughout the book are level unless otherwise stated. Use a set of measuring spoons for accurate measuring.

All eggs used in the recipes are large unless otherwise stated.

## VOLUMES

| METRIC | IMPERIAL |
| --- | --- |
| 25ml | 1fl oz |
| 50ml | 2fl oz |
| 75ml | 3fl oz |
| 100ml | 3½fl oz |
| 150ml | 5fl oz (¼ pint) |
| 200ml | 7fl oz |
| 300ml | 10fl oz (½ pint) |
| 450ml | 15fl oz (¾ pint) |
| 600ml | 1 pint |
| 700ml | 1¼ pints |
| 900ml | 1½ pints |
| 1 litre | 1¾ pints |
| 1.1 litres | 2 pints |
| 1.3 litres | 2¼ pints |
| 1.5 litres | 2½ pints |
| 1.6 litres | 2¾ pints |
| 1.75 litres | 3 pints |
| 1.8 litres | 3¼ pints |
| 2 litres | 3½ pints |
| 2.1 litres | 3¾ pints |
| 2.25 litres | 4 pints |
| 3 litres | 5 pints |
| 3.5 litres | 6 pints |

## WEIGHTS

| METRIC | IMPERIAL |
| --- | --- |
| 15g | ½oz |
| 25g | 1oz |
| 40g | 1½oz |
| 50g | 2oz |
| 75g | 3oz |
| 100g | 4oz |
| 150g | 5oz |
| 175g | 6oz |
| 200g | 7oz |
| 225g | 8oz |
| 250g | 9oz |
| 275g | 10oz |
| 300g | 11oz |
| 350g | 12oz |
| 375g | 13oz |
| 400g | 14oz |
| 425g | 15oz |
| 450g | 1lb |
| 550g | 1¼lb |
| 700g | 1½lb |
| 800g | 1¾lb |

# INDEX

creamy roasted pepper pasta with feta and
    olives 166
freezing 307
giant cheese and Parma ham straws 19
herb flatbread with mozzarella and
    asparagus 12
hot turkey and avocado bake 109
Mexican tortilla bake 135
party ploughman's 16
pork, apple and Stilton parcels 116
pork chops with mushroom crust 119
roasted vegetable quiche 178–80
turkey Waldorf salad 106
watermelon, feta and mint stacks 26
see also cream cheese; goat's cheese;
    mascarpone
cherries (glacé)
    chocolate and cherry biscuits 287
    fruitcake loaves 273
chicken 104–5
    chicken and bacon lattice pie 89–91
    chicken cordon bleu 92
    chicken noodle laksa 46
    chicken, red wine and garlic casserole 100
    chicken schnitzel with fried egg 95
    smoked Texan chicken wings 87
    spiced chicken skewers with tzatziki 84
    stock 105
    stuffed chicken thighs with lemon sauce 96
    Thai chicken curry 99
    whole roast chicken with lemon and
        herbs 103
chickpeas
    Middle Eastern aubergine and chickpea
        salad 181
chillies
    roasted aubergine and garlic chilli dip 29
chocolate 226
    bonfire chocolate traybake 280
    cardamom sponge with white chocolate
        icing 277–8
    chocolate and cherry biscuits 287
    ginger and white chocolate florentines 289
    mini chocolate tarts 258
    red velvet cupcakes 283
    white chocolate ice cream 221
chowder, smoked haddock and sweetcorn 67
cobbler, apple and blackberry 264
coconut
    cranberry and coconut energy bars 294
    gluten-free apple and coconut cake 269
coconut milk
    chicken noodle laksa 46
coffee
    latte panna cotta 237
coleslaw, rainbow 209

continental sharing platter 18
coulibiac, salmon and herb 65–6
courgettes
    garden tagliatelle 158
    posh roasted vegetables 200
    spiralized vegetables 207
crab quenelles with samphire 57
crackling 139
cranberry and coconut energy bars 294
crayfish
    crayfish marinière on sourdough 49
    oriental vegetable and noodle salad 176
cream
    blackberry ripple 222
    freezing 307
    latte panna cotta 237
    mango, lemon and lime mousse 215
    passion fruit pots 212
    see also custard; ice cream
cream cheese
    red pepper dip 18
    salmon fillets with herbs and red
        pepper 68
crème brûlée tart 261–3
crème caramel 234
croutons 175
cucumber
    smoked salmon, avocado and
        cucumber canapés 25
    tzatziki 84
curry
    curried beetroot soup 48
    Thai chicken curry 99
custard 227
    brioche bread and butter pudding 240
    crème brûlée tart 261–3
    crème caramel 234

D
desserts, foolproof 226–7
dips
    red pepper dip 18
    roasted aubergine and garlic chilli dip 29
    tzatziki 84

E
eggs
    chicken schnitzel with fried egg 95
    freezing 308
elderflower cordial
    lemon and elderflower jellies 216
en papillote, fish 72
energy bars, cranberry and coconut 294
entertaining, foolproof 312–13
Eve's pudding, rhubarb 243

F
fennel
    salmon, fennel and pea risotto 168
fish 70–2
    all-in-one fish gratin 80
    freezing 306
    see also monkfish, salmon etc
flageolet beans, slow-roast shoulder of lamb
    with 147–9
florentines, ginger and white chocolate 289
foolproof tips
    bread 38–40
    cakes 284–6
    desserts 226–7
    entertaining 312–13
    family food 310–11
    fish 70–2
    freezing 306–9
    meat 138–40
    pasta and rice 162–4
    pastry 250–1
    poultry 104–5
    salads and vegetables 196–9
    store cupboards 304–5
frangipane tart 246
freezing 306–9
fruit
    freezing 306–7
    see also apples, bananas etc
fruit cakes
    Easter Simnel cake 279
    fruitcake loaves 273
frying meat 139–40

G
game bolognaise 113
gammon with mustard and orange sauce 125
garden tagliatelle 158
garlic
    cheese and garlic tear-and-share scones 34
    garlic crushed new potatoes 194
    roasted aubergine and garlic chilli dip 29
    tarragon aioli 54
gateau, summer party 219–20
gelatine 226–7
ginger
    ginger and white chocolate
        florentines 289
    ginger semifreddo with poached
        pears 233
    stem ginger shortbread 297
goat's cheese
    tomato and basil salad with whipped goat's
        cheese and Parma ham 15
gratin, all-in-one fish 80
gravy 122

# THANK YOU

I am extremely fortunate to be supported by such wonderful people – a truly foolproof team! Lucy Young is the powerhouse behind me and my work. After 26 years together we think completely alike. She has exceptional culinary skills and patience, and we all love and admire her.

**PUBLISHING TEAM** We are so thrilled with this book, so thanks to Ebury and BBC Books for commissioning it! Lizzy Gray and Kate Fox, with Lucy Jessop, Kate Parker and Lucy Stephens, are a lovely publishing team who have designed and created this book with such skill and dedication. The book is a wonderful reflection of the TV series giving every recipe detail to the home cook.

**FOODIE TEAM** The wonderful Lisa Harrison and Isla Murray were on set for the book *and* the TV series, which is a joy for me – they are so talented. Wonderfully talented and very lovely Georgia Glynn Smith, who photographed every photo in the book, ably assisted by the ever-so-cheeky Bobby Goulding, and Sophie Fox. Thanks too to Liz Belton for the gorgeous props and styling, and to Jo Penford who makes me look 'camera ready' in an hour. Jo, you are amazing and I'm sorry I fidget so much!

**TV TEAM** Shine Soho have done an amazing job producing the television series which accompanies the book. Special thanks to Karen Ross, David Ambler, Emma Boswell and all the wonderful crew. Lucy and I enjoyed every day, we truly admire their expertise and couldn't have asked for more – big thanks!

**HOME TEAM** Lovely Lucinda McCord who is with me and Lucy testing the recipes – all my testing is done at home, making tasting time the highlight of the day! She is such a brilliant cook and mother of two. And thanks to Kathryn Demery who works in the office part-time dealing with letters, letters and more letters!

Thank you all

Love Mary x